God Bless You Laurie
Evelyn Leite 2022

Praise for *Women: What Do We Want?*

This book can change your life!! I loved this book! I had to make myself slow down because I couldn't wait to read and learn more! I saw every woman I've ever known and wanted to take this book right to each one of them. I ended up buying a number of them and have a check list for more. It is so intriguing because the author zeros in on exactly how to define what you want.
Mia A (as posted on Amazon review)

Reading this book made me angry. Not at the author but at the things she describes women are still going through. I ended up buying 10 copies of it and giving one to every member of my family, there is so much wisdom in this book and thoughts that I could never put into words for them
Bill B.

The first thing I did after reading this book was give it to my daughter, maybe that's the most concise and and meaningful complement I can give. With out losing any speed, cover to cover the author goes right to the point in every chapter and who better to tell the story of human emotional entanglements and to unravel them with such simple clarity than a therapist who has heard them over and over ad-infinitum.
Sherry (as posted on Amazon)

This book has been a long time coming. The author included material for women and men too, that needed to be brought out into the open. The stories the women told were so real —one that keeps playing in my head is a woman telling about her husband treating their dog better than he treats her. This book gives voice to those needing to be heard. I could see parts of myself especially when I wasn't able to ask directly for what I needed, nor believed I deserved to be treated respectfully. I gave a copy to a friend and she loved it.
Delaine

Before I read this book I was struggling, I wondered if there was something wrong with me because I was having so many problems in my marriage. I gave it to my husband and it opened up discussions and the results of being able to communicate helped both of us to have a closer relationship.
Tracey L

WOMEN
What Do We Want?

CHANGING YOUR LIFE IS EASIER THAN YOU THINK

WOMEN
What Do We Want?

CHANGING YOUR LIFE IS EASIER THAN YOU THINK

REAL STORIES OF THE SEXUAL, SPIRITUAL
AND EMOTIONAL EXPERIENCES OF WOMEN

Evelyn Leite, MHR, LPC

Living With Solutions Press
RAPID CITY, SOUTH DAKOTA

Women: What Do We Want? Changing Your Life Is Easier Than You Think / Evelyn Leite. —2nd ed.

Copyright © 2016 by Evelyn Leite

All rights reserved. No part of this publication may be reproduced, distributed or transmitted in any form or by any means, including photocopying, recording, or other electronic or mechanical methods, without the prior written permission of the publisher, except in the case of brief quotations embodied in critical reviews and certain other noncommercial uses permitted by copyright law. For permission requests, write to the publisher, addressed "Attention: Permissions Coordinator," at

Living With Solutions
P. O. Box 9702
Rapid City, South Dakota 57709
www.livingwithsolutions.biz

Ordering Information. Quantity sales. Special discounts are available on quantity purchases by corporations, associations, and others. For details, contact the "Special Sales Department" at the address above.

ISBN 978-1-945333-00-2

Published in the United States of America by Living With Solutions Press

Contents

ACKNOWLEDGEMENTS vii
DEDICATION ix
INTRODUCTION xi

Section One: For Women Who Dare...To Ask For More

1 Does it even matter what women want? 3
2 Do you know what you want and are you getting it? 7
3 Say good-by to loneliness 11
4 Men who can't give you what you want 15
5 The kind of love no woman wants 27
6 Jealousy leaves everyone wanting 31
7 The media tells us what we want 35
8 The woman who wants more and better sex 39
9 A woman with class gets what she wants 47
10 A real problem in getting what you want 49

Section Two: For Men Who Want to Know How to Please a Woman

11 The woman who wants too much of you 55
12 Women! You can't live with them, and you can't live without them. 59
13 Have you ever asked yourself what you want? 65
14 Men want love too 69
15 Women want men with class 73
16 Foreplay: the mark of a masterful lover 77
17 What women say they want from their men 81

Section Three: Real Women, Real Stories 85

Postscript
On a scale of 1 to 10, what's your chance of getting what you want? 123

ACKNOWLEDGEMENTS

Writing is a difficult and solitary life. I could not have finished this book without my amazingly patient, loving husband. He is a real trooper who inspires me and supports me emotionally and physically while I toil to make a difference.

I wish to thank my three sons for being stalwart, gentle, God-fearing men who put so much joy in my life. They continually support and encourage me during the long and sometimes lonesome roads I travel.

Thanks also to all my friends, Suzan Nolan, Judy Jones, Ron Comes, Lin Jennewein, George Lindahl, Tracey Wright-Belk and Laura Keyser, who read the manuscript and gave comments and support, and to Marj Hahne and Karen Hall, my editors, who patiently worked through this material with me.

My undying gratitude to Delaine Shay and Ron Wick to whom I am much in debt for their continuing validation of my efforts.

I especially wish to applaud and acknowledge all the brave women who continue to fight the stereotypes and who contributed their stories for the benefit of others.

DEDICATION

I dedicate this book to my mother, who faced all the obstacles that a woman born in the early 1900s encountered. She was light years ahead of her time, and the bravest woman I know. Her soft voice, her gentle hands, her steadfast belief in God, her generosity and her wisdom are my guiding lights.

While some of you might be surprised at the frank sexual content in this book, my mother would nod wisely because she is the one who told me that "sex is a beautiful thing and given by God for us to enjoy when we get married." (This was the sum total of our sex talk. Hey, it could've been a lot worse.) Though this was her stance with me, she was incredibly supportive of friends and family who got pregnant outside of marriage.

INTRODUCTION

Sigmund Freud, the founder of the psychoanalytic school of psychology, was—and still is—highly respected for his groundbreaking work in understanding the human psyche. Freud determined many things about human nature and the subconscious mind. He was the first psychiatrist to believe that the repression of emotions hampers the natural development of children, and he was the first to understand the profound significance of dreams. He normalized behaviors that other people of his day thought were psychotic. Freud was vitally interested in sexual matters and coined the term "penis envy," believing that women deliberately thwarted men because they envied them. He studied women's behavior intently but their conduct remained an enigma to him.

History tells us that Freud was dumbfounded by the power women had over him. He believed that men have superior intelligence and that he, a renowned psychiatrist, should be able to figure out such simple-minded beings. He was perplexed and frustrated to find that women did not fit into his preconceived notions.

Freud was an object both of wonder and disdain in my college psychology and social work classes. I am a licensed Professional Counselor and a member of The American Association of Sex Educators and Therapists. I'm blessed and privileged to have known and worked with a wide variety of people, many of them clients, for over thirty years. I hear stories of heartbreak and suffering from both men and women, and most of what I hear concerns relationships. I do not counsel people who are happy, productive and contented. As a result, this book deals with people who are questioning the very meaning of their existence. The bulk of my client load is comprised of women in bad relationships, which means that, for each woman, there is also a man in a bad relationship who is most likely wondering what the hell is happening.

In preparation for this book, I asked women, "What do you want—physically—spiritually—emotionally—sexually?" This is an interesting venture into the feminine soul. Women looked distrustfully at me and were dubious about the question; some giggled like schoolgirls, some gave an angry response and some looked sideways and said, "I have to think about it."

Freud's question—what do women want—frustrates men. The problem is, it also frustrates women. When I ask a woman what she wants, she usually stares at me with a blank look on her face, then hems and haws for a while. Sometimes she explodes in a volley of rhetoric that tells me what she doesn't want, or she says, "Can I get back to you on this?" Many of the women in my family and some of my close friends would not even go near the subject of what they want and need to feel fulfilled. They self-consciously laughed off the questions; a couple of them even looked at their husbands and said, "You tell her what I want." One of my friends crossed me off her friend list when she discovered that my list of questions included the subject of sexual satisfaction.

This no-holds-barred book talks frankly about relationships and contains real stories of woman's sexual, spiritual and emotional experiences. It divulges everything women tell me they want. Here is a secret I learned in this process: what women want can't be purchased. In fact, in talking with some of them I hear, "I could hire everything done that he does. Why can't I get him to understand what is really important?" Women are hurting and disillusioned in relationships primarily because of gross misunderstandings. Communication sometimes becomes impossible because of perceived rules and conventions passed down from previous generations.

When I told my male acquaintances that I was writing a book about what women want, every single one of them said, "I'll buy the first copy." In my experience, most men really do want to please women, they just aren't always capable of hearing what we have to say. Men often tune women out because what they're expressing is not that significant to a man. The men I've questioned about this allude to fear, exhaustion, superiority and disinterest. One man said, "I pretend like I'm interested but I don't actually know what she's talking about." Another man said, "Why do women have to talk everything to death anyway?"

I hope this book will enable men and women to come to a deeper understanding of their God-given value, and alleviate some of the frustration and anger that arises from lack of understanding or poor communication skills. Please read it with an eye to improving your relationship, first with yourself and then with others.

SECTION ONE

For Women

WHO DARE...TO ASK FOR MORE

Chapter 1

Does it even matter what women want?

We've come a long way, baby...or have we? We are doctors, lawyers, ministers, psychologists, engineers, teachers and CEOs of big companies. We are waitresses, clerks, childcare workers and stay-at-home mothers. Many of us are like the proverbial duck, appearing self-assured and well put together on the surface but, underneath, paddling like crazy to stay afloat.

In my work the number one issue is relationships. The anticipation of a "happily ever after" relationship and the resulting disappointment in the lack of healthy connection has women suffering from anger, depression, anxiety, shame and guilt. Some of you are grieving a loss of identity; some of you are dealing with wearisome sexual issues and many of you have little or no sense of being significant.

It is hard for a woman to understand and respect her value if, as a child, no one told her of her worth. Such a woman tends to allow men to define her and, if the definition is made with abuse or neglect, she lives accordingly. Even a woman who is aware of her significance can lose her sense of meaning if she connects with the wrong man.

Some women are uncertain about their right to want more out of life. They express feelings of disappointment or emptiness, and I hear these excuses:

"There is no money. My husband wouldn't like it. The other people at work would make my life hell. People would talk about me. I can't leave here." And, of course, "Who is going to take care of my children?" They discourage themselves from going after what they want because they fear there will be a huge emotional price to pay. They fear abandonment by the very people who profess to care about them.

Women are angry—and many do not even know it. Many women blame men for their feelings of being trapped and unfulfilled. And it is true that in many ways women are forced to be subordinate to men. My generation has tried hard to bring attention to gender inequality and we have made great strides; however, there is much to accomplish in personal attitudes and mindsets to overcome the legacy of subservience passed down from mothers, grandmothers, aunts and religious leaders.

In the 1950s and 1960s, what women wanted was not important. Our most important job was taking care of our husbands and children or our aging parents. Girls who expressed a desire to have a career were often the butts of jokes. Waitress, secretary, teacher, nurse or other serving roles were assigned to women, and this was just to keep us busy until we could get to the real stuff: marriage, home, children and white picket fence.

I was extremely fortunate that my father insisted that I must go to college at a time when many girls did not even go to high school. I didn't, though. I bowed to my mother's desire that I set up housekeeping and get married while still in high school. College came much later—after thirteen years in the school of hard knocks.

Girls and boys in the 1950s learned from the generations before them that there are two kinds of women: the kind you marry and the kind you enjoy carnally. The kind you marry were virgins, and all the others were sluts, whores or spinsters. In those days, when a woman was raped, she was better off dead because she was considered damaged goods and no one would want to marry her. The whispers about rape usually blamed the female, as did judges and juries. Have we come very far?

In the fifties and sixties, parents carried around an inordinate amount of shame concerning their children's sexual activities. Girls disappeared from school—there one day, gone the next—because parents sent pregnant girls into hiding. Girls and boys of fifteen and sixteen were forced to get married to protect their parents' reputations. The father of one of my friends beat his pregnant sixteen-year-old daughter within an inch of her life, and this was the rule rather than the exception in the small town where I grew up.

The following is an excerpt from a 1950s Home Economics high school textbook[1]. It clearly shows how women were regarded then—and how much has changed.

- HAVE DINNER READY. Plan, even the night before, to have a delicious meal ready on time for his return. This is a way of letting him know that you have been thinking about him and are concerned about his needs. Most men are hungry when they get home and the prospect of a good meal is part of the warm welcome needed.
- PREPARE YOURSELF. Take 15 minutes to rest so you will be refreshed when he arrives. Touch up your make-up, put a ribbon in your hair and be fresh looking. He has just been with a lot of work weary people.
- BE A LITTLE GAY AND A LITTLE MORE INTERESTING FOR HIM. His boring day may need a lift and one of your duties is to provide it.
- CLEAR AWAY THE CLUTTER. Make one last trip through the main part of the house just before your husband arrives. Run a dust cloth over the tables.
- IN THE COOLER MONTHS OF THE YEAR, YOU SHOULD PREPARE AND LIGHT A FIRE FOR HIM TO UNWIND BY. Your husband will feel he has reached a haven of rest and order, and it will give you a lift, too. After all, catering to his comfort will provide you with immense personal satisfaction.
- MINIMIZE ALL NOISE. At the time of his arrival, eliminate all noise of the washer, dryer or vacuum. Encourage the children to be quiet.
- BE HAPPY TO SEE HIM.
- GREET HIM WITH A WARM SMILE AND SHOW SINCERITY IN YOUR DESIRE TO PLEASE HIM.

---

[1] Reprinted in *Housekeeping Monthly*, 13 May 1955.

- LISTEN TO HIM. You may have a dozen important things to tell him, but the moment of his arrival is not the time. Let him talk first—remember his topics of conversation are more important that yours.
- DON'T GREET HIM WITH COMPLAINTS AND PROBLEMS.
- DON'T COMPLAIN IF HE IS LATE FOR DINNER OR EVEN IF HE STAYS OUT ALL NIGHT. Count this as minor compared to what he might have gone through at work.
- MAKE HIM COMFORTABLE. Have him lean back in a comfortable chair or lie him down in the bedroom. Have a cool or warm drink ready for him.
- ARRANGE HIS PILLOW AND OFFER TO TAKE OFF HIS SHOES. Speak in a low, soothing and pleasant voice.
- DON'T ASK HIM QUESTIONS ABOUT HIS ACTIONS OR QUESTION HIS JUDGMENT OR INTEGRITY. Remember he is the master of the house and as such will always exercise his will with fairness and truthfulness. You have no right to question him.
- A GOOD WIFE ALWAYS KNOWS HER PLACE.

Women and girls were handed many rules and few choices. Those who questioned the status quo were treated poorly and accused of being bitches, dykes, ballbreakers and/or troublemakers. I still occasionally hear those names. And when men really admire a woman for being smart, capable, savvy and enterprising, I hear them say, "She's got balls."

Recently (2013) I was watching a talk show on TV. A single, young male celebrity was responding to a question about his love life and he said, "If she is beautiful, I will go after her. If she has a brain, that is frosting on the cake." He then said, "I have enough brains for both of us." Who raised this man? What are his chances for an equitable relationship and could any woman really feel connected to him? We have come far in many ways, but we still have a long way to go.

CHAPTER 2

Do you know what you want and are you getting it?

I've interviewed hundreds of you. When I ask you to tell me about yourself, you identify yourself by what you do and the roles you play. I am a mother, a wife, a girlfriend, a sister, a daughter, a teacher, a counselor, a clerk, a doctor, a lawyer. It usually takes a lot of prodding and much encouragement to get you to explore your values and your deepest wants and needs. "Who are you?" I say repeatedly, until some of you get angry with me for not accepting that you are what you do. Many of you judge yourselves by the man you are with or the one you have lost. You gauge your worth by your romantic entanglements or by your social position. You live with the incongruity of having to be one person at work and an entirely different person at home. You work and go to school and take care of children. Some of you are single, some of you have husbands who support you, some of you have husbands who abuse you emotionally and physically. Some of you are single mothers with several children by different fathers. All of you struggle to make the best of your life.

When discussing relationships you find it easy to generalize your dissatisfaction, usually accompanied by tears. You frequently apologize and try to stifle the overflowing feelings. You find it hard to put your pain into words.

You are not used to being heard.

You have spent years learning to say what people want to hear. You deny and reject your own thoughts and feelings to keep the peace, keep the man or keep the job. You have learned to get your needs met with seduction, manipulation, clues, signals, hints and emotional blackmail. Some of you quietly smoke pot or drink yourselves to sleep at night so you won't have to deal with the situation in which you find yourself.

By the time I see you, there are tears, heartache and anger. If your significant other is with you, it is hard to say what must be said because you fear sounding stupid, or fear that he will abandon or punish you once you leave my office. The details are spit out bitterly because you have kept them bottled up for so long. As you express your dissatisfaction and the lack of fulfillment you feel, he acts confused and has a "who me?" look on his face.

"What do you want from him?" I ask you.

"I want him to treat me better."

"What does 'better' mean?"

"Yeah," he growls, "what does it mean?"

"Paint me a picture with words," I say, "so I can understand. Say exactly what you want."

The torrent of hurt pours out. "He knows what I want! I have said it often enough."

By now, he's giving you a look that says, "When?"

As you talk, the look changes to, "When hell freezes over."

He's got a story of his own and he wants it heard. He does not want to be wrong. And you know for certain that you are right. But honestly, what is right is that you must share your story, he must share his, and each much accept the validity of the other's experience.

You think that you are unique in your failures, but I know you to be extremely strong, tough and valiant. You have been through many trials and disappointments. Your troubles didn't crush you, they made you stronger. You have a drive for fulfillment. You know that you must either keep on progressing or die emotionally—and sometimes physically. What you want is for your mate to understand the feelings you have.

When you tell him what you want simply and clearly, he does one of three things:

- ridicule you with sarcasm,
- swear he has never heard it before, or
- acknowledge that he is part of the problem.

There is little hope for a relationship when ridicule and sarcasm are present. Ridicule and sarcasm kill your spirit and are the tools of a bully. Many men are verbally abusive without knowing it. Some are deliberately trying to hurt you. They might be suffering from anxiety, stress, and physical overload, but do not excuse this behavior. Patricia Evans has published a great book, titled The Verbally Abusive Relationship, that I often recommend to my clients. It gives good clear directions and maps out coping skills.

When a man looks you in the eye and swears that he has never heard your complaint before, don't assume he lying. Instead, assume he tunes you out and he really never has heard it before. You have tolerated this behavior because you don't know how to make him hear you. There are some communication techniques in this book that will help you to be heard. The most important thing, though, is to assume that you need to present your information in a way that he understands. Often this means the time for talk is over and now action is required.

If your man chooses the third response—accepts that he is part of the problem—and offers to make some changes, especially if he follows through on those changes, keep him. He's a good man. Give him time. Be willing to allow yourself time to make changes also.

CHAPTER 3

Say good-by to loneliness

Loneliness is the number one complaint of women. By the time I meet with a woman there has been much suffering. The disillusionments, the traumatic childhoods, the emotional neglect and the lack of preparation for choosing relationships wisely have left them bitter, angry and cynical. While they share self-reproach and feelings of failure, I marvel at their courage. I see an attractive woman who has no sense of her beauty or her value as a human being. She doesn't know how brave she is or how valiant she appears to me. She always expresses profound relief when I tell her that she is not crazy and her life really does suck.

When I ask women to be specific about what they need to be happy, they say they want to be "loved, adored, appreciated, encouraged, understood, recognized as special, courted, wooed, listened to and heard" by the men in their lives. Many are in love-hate relationships and have not been able to discuss any topic with their significant other for a long time. Talk of money turns into a war of words. Discussions about sex end in frustration. Battles over who is right and fights over ways to discipline children leave them exhausted.

Sometimes when a woman finally comes for help, she is not currently in a relationship. Choosing the right man has proven to be problematic. She openly wonders, "What is wrong with me?" She thinks it is her fault that her relationships have failed. She complains, "All the good men are either married or gay," not realizing that "good" men are everywhere. She has just been looking in the wrong place—and with the wrong attitude.

It is wonderful to have a relationship with the right man. If he is the right man, a woman will be with him for healthy reasons—his emotional availability and willingness to bond. However, even in the twenty-first century, a secret Cinderella is very much alive in some of us. Many women still want to be rescued by Prince Charming from a life of loneliness or tediousness. They don't realize that their loneliness is coming from a big empty hole where a sense of self worth should be. This hole can't be filled by a man, by a child or by food, alcohol or drugs.

Loneliness can cause highly educated women to toss their budding careers aside for a man. I am amazed at the number of women who abandon the rights other women have worked so hard to secure for them and bow to a man's supposed superiority. With an "I hate it, but I can't help it" attitude, women deny themselves the promise of their birthright to please a man, often one who is alcoholic, drug addicted, emotionally abusive or just plain self-centered. Their self-worth is pretty much nonexistent. Here is the veiled truth: a woman in this kind of relationship believes it is her job as a woman to fix him.

Women are taught that men are "fixable," so when she can't fix him she feels like a failure. All that old rhetoric about "the woman behind the man" causes a woman to think she has more power than she actually does. And what about the woman who is in a "good" relationship with a dependable, steadfast man but is bored to tears by the lack of excitement and the inertia of the living room recliner? Her loneliness fills her with guilt as she daydreams of a more exciting life. Perhaps she'll have an affair with an exciting someone who really appreciates her. There is a reason why romance novels are constantly in demand. Their popularity speaks to the rapacious yearning women have for romance.

When a woman feels trapped, it might be because of her unwillingness to rock the boat or to take chances. When a woman is uncertain about making demands or claiming her right to feel fulfilled, or if she has tunnel vision because of lack of money, exhaustion, demanding jobs or children for whom she must provide, she might not reach out or be able to see her options. She must honestly explore all available possibilities with the help of someone who can see them more clearly. She must realize that a man is not a panacea, and he contains no magic formulas. Any ability he has to take away her emptiness is temporary.

A lonely woman must accept that her biggest problem is attitude. Only she can make the decision to fill her own emptiness, and there are many ways to do it. Virginia Satir, a wonderful therapist, taught me the three M's of contentment.

Music

Music, for me, means dancing as well as listening, and is one of the elixirs that make life worthwhile. In fact, I would rather dance than eat.

Massage

Massage fills our need for the healing, soothing touch that many of us are missing at home. Be selective about the massage therapist; some are actual healers and more capable than others, like my friend Betty Lambert who can truly make the world go away for a while with her restorative touch.

Masturbation

Masturbation is a great tool for satisfaction when sexual intercourse is not an option and neither is an affair. It provides sexual healing and is a secret formula for warm, strong, self-pleasure that satisfies the desire for an exquisite experience. It allows you to learn more about who you are and what heights you can reach.

In order to conquer loneliness, a woman must expand her imagination, stop worrying about what other people might say about her and reach for her dreams. She must give herself permission to stretch her limits and blow her original archetypes wide open. She must stop trying to be all things to all people. A resourceful woman can find ways to take care of herself once she gives herself permission to search through the rummage of her paralyzing beliefs. But first, she must accept the truth of what Walter Kelly's Pogo says in his comic strip: "I have met the enemy and it is me."

CHAPTER 4

Men who can't give you what you want

You are very clear that you want a meaningful and fulfilling love relationship. One of the problems I see often is that you are trying to have it with someone who is not capable of giving it to you. The following descriptions could help you discern if you are in a relationship worth saving or possibly stop you from getting involved in one that simply kills your spirit.

The Passive-Aggressive Man

The passive-aggressive man knows how to be charming, how to lie by omission about who he really is and how to pretend that he has no expectations of you. This man, on the surface, appears to be quiet, mild mannered, modest, generous and peace seeking. All your friends see him as such. Just below the surface of this persona, however, is bitterness, sulking, scorn, blaming, stubbornness, resentment, pouting and fear of intimacy. You do not understand what is going on with him, so much of the time you feel crazy and confused. You question yourself. You wonder what is wrong—do you really deserve this treatment? You did not mean to upset him, so why is he giving you the silent treatment—or is he? You can't be sure.

The passive aggressive person believes his unhappiness is your fault. You have failed him in some way, but he does not have the courage to be honest with you about it so he resorts to subterfuge and sabotage. Instead of talking directly with you, he grunts or stares into space. When he talks, it is behind your back with someone else. Or he picks a time when others are around to make mean-spirited remarks. Sometimes he sinks into self-pity, which is often diagnosed as depression.

This man lost his voice in childhood when it was not safe to express feelings or dissatisfaction to an adult. The people who raised him have rendered him gutless. He now gets his power from being the only one who knows what is going on. Knowledge is power in a relationship, and secrets and hidden agendas are the weapons of those who feel powerless. If you are in a relationship with this man, he rarely tells you how he feels, will not give you information that is important for you to know, sabotages your efforts to accomplish a task, often shows up late, ridicules you and makes mean remarks about things important to you.

Passive-aggressive men create constant insecurity in you by quietly resisting routine social and relational obligations and insinuating there is something wrong with you. He forgets important occasions or dresses shabbily when the occasion calls for classy attire, and acts innocent when he ruins a special event for you. If you are excited or joyful over something, negative comments or looks of scorn dampen your enthusiasm. If you like something, he will hate it. When he gives you a gift, it will be something you don't want; never mind that you might have pointed out to him many times something that you do want.

Such a person is miserable most of the time because he goes unheard, and he is not heard because he doesn't say anything that anyone can understand. Silence speaks volumes but it is impossible to interpret, and one should never even try. Out of the blue, a passive-aggressive man (who has at his core a denied, submerged, disowned rage) blames you for things you have never even thought of doing—and he feels justified in doing so. He keeps you guessing about what he wants and sets up barriers to stop you from having what you want. If he knows something will make you happy, he will not do it or will do it resentfully. He pulls you into his chaotic sense of dissatisfaction with everything around him by making jibes or negative cracks about people, places and things. His world is small because he deliberately eliminates anything he cannot control or predict. Terry Kellog, a colleague of mine, defines passive-aggressive behavior as "a big dog simultaneously licking your face and peeing on your shoes."

The passive-aggressive man often withholds sex as a way of punishment. In extreme cases, he will go and have sex with someone else. He will let his partner think it is because she is not attractive enough and he will be silent while she blames herself for what is happening. A client's husband told her he could not maintain an erection because he was not physically attracted to her. Only women who have very high self-esteem can resist believing that they must not be attractive or desirable if he avoids having sex with her. (If a man cannot maintain an erection or avoids sex, it has nothing to do with his partner and everything to do with his mental or physical health.) Even women who have high self-esteem have to work very hard to maintain it when living with a passive aggressive man.

If you love this person, confront his behavior. Assure him that you can handle the truth. Tell him you can hear only what he says, not what he does not say. Tell him in a calm, quiet manner how his behavior makes you feel and then encourage him to share his feelings. He does not know how to express himself, so model effective communication for him. If he escalates in angry blame and accusations, table the conversation and tell him that when he can speak calmly, you will talk again. Give him as many chances as he needs to get it right if he is willing to try. He learned this behavior and he can unlearn it.[2]

Cindy and Ralph

Cindy is in a relationship with a chubby, hale, hearty, easygoing kind of a guy. She fell in love with his seeming chivalrous, polite behavior; at times, he could even be gallant. He has a way with people that she lacks, is popular and fun to be around. Everybody likes him, while most people who know her think she is too outspoken. Ralph never says anything when he disagrees with their friends, or when the mechanic that works on his car overcharges him or when the paperboy forgets to leave the paper. But Cindy notices that the mechanic has to bill him three or four times before he will write the check, even though money is not an issue. She hears him talk about how mistaken his friends are behind their backs, and notices that the paper boy has had a couple of bicycle tires go flat right in front of their house.

She often gets exasperated with Ralph because he never tells her what he wants even when she asks. In the beginning she used to plead, "What's wrong?" but since she never got an answer, she finally gave up and now just endures

---

[2] For more information on passive-aggressiveness read, Living With The Passive Aggressive Man, by Scott Wetzler, Ph.D.

the silent treatment. Cindy is so involved in her own life that sometimes she doesn't even realize she's getting the silent treatment until it becomes painfully obvious that when she tries to engage him in conversation, he answers in one or two words or not at all. In addition to this, he "forgets" a lot of things that she thinks are important. Sometimes they go weeks without sex and even though she asks him about it, she never gets a satisfactory answer. Recently he was upset with their nine-year-old son because he used Ralph's screwdriver to fix his bike and left it laying in the yard. He sent their son out to look for it and after the boy had searched the yard for a long time, Cindy noticed that Ralph had the screwdriver in his back pocket.

"Why?" she asked.

"To teach him a lesson," he said.

The Narcissistic Man

The narcissistic man does not have the capacity to move beyond his own self-absorbed, egotistical world. Everything he does is to make himself look good to him. In the world of a narcissist, people are completely unimportant except as a way for him to get his needs met. Narcissists at their core are cold, cruel, and empty. Either doting parents who thought he could do no wrong raised him or, hiding deep underneath the vacuum that is his spirit, lies unresolved heartache that occurred when he was quite small and he is stuck in the trauma.

He is capable of switching at the drop of a hat from a good guy to a bad guy. He may be handsome and appear to be kind and loving. However, once you are in relationship with him, the message he gives you is, "Please me and I will love you. Displease me and you are dirt."

For those of you who love a narcissist, any idea of reciprocation is fantasy. A narcissist does not love. He is emotionally dependent; he needs you, but he does not love you. He is a self-centered person who uses "I," "me" and "my" in every sentence. He thinks no one in the world is as smart as he is and because of this, he cannot stand to lose at anything. He can't ever admit to being wrong and will never apologize if he hurts you—unless he must do this to get something he wants. Whatever he does, he has to be the best at doing it or he will quit. If you beat him at anything, or if he sees that other people are better at doing something than he is, he will profess to hate doing it.

The narcissist considers everything in the light of how it affects his comfort. He launches into talking about himself the minute you ask the question, "How are you?" He rarely or never asks about you or what is going on in your life, unless he is seeking information for some devious purpose of his own. If he must think of you and what you want (in order to look good), he will make you pay. Any nurture and support you might get from him is for a selfish reason, such as, "I will flatter you and profess my love so you will have sex with me." He thinks himself unique and above the rules that govern other people. Narcissists do not do well in therapy because their only goal is to outwit the therapist.

Darlene and Jacob

Jacob, 36, a well-educated professional, is a narcissist of the worst kind. Darlene has noticed that every action, every thought he has, is about him and how others perceive him. In the beginning of their relationship she was enamored with his quick wit, his charming good looks and the chemistry that sizzled between them. Tall and beautiful herself, she didn't realize that he only needed her to make him look good.

Now married to Jacob, she no longer feels special or important, just tired most of the time. Unwittingly she has becomes an extension of who he is. He believes that she must reflect perfectly on him or others will think he married somebody who brings him down, makes him less than perfect. He doesn't care at all how she feels about herself, only how others feel about her. He believes that the way she looks is a reflection of his worth. So he encourages her to buy new clothes, get her hair cut, and wear three-inch heels. He makes sure that he wears only the best, and checks himself in the mirror every time he walks by one.

When they are invited to a large company Christmas party, Jacob takes his time to get ready and then waits impatiently for Darlene, who had to wait for him to vacate the bathroom. When she finally comes down the stairs, he takes one look at her, grimaces and says, "You're not wearing that, are you?"

Darlene's heart plummets and she suddenly feels ugly. Struggling to hold back the tears, she says, "What shall I wear, then?" Treating her as if she is an idiot, Jacob goes to her closet and picks out a low cut black sheath that is guaranteed to make Darlene suck in her stomach and feel uncomfortable all night. She lets him control her, down to the color of eye shadow she wears, and whether or not she carries a purse.

When they get to the party, Darlene is dressed as Jacob has directed her. Jacob fills his cocktail plate with barbecued ribs, but admonishes Darlene not to eat anything because she's getting fat. This comment stings her to the core but to preserve the peace she nibbles on a piece of celery. When Jacob bites into one of the ribs, he chips a tooth slightly on a particularly hard bone.

"We have to leave," he tells Darlene who is deep in conversation with an acquaintance.

"Why?"

"Because I chipped my tooth. Everyone will notice."

"Honey, they won't. I can't even tell, and I'm standing right in front of you."

"Well, I can tell. Let's go." He drags her to the coatroom and, fuming, won't talk to her all the way home. Somehow, this is her fault although she does not fathom how.

When they get home he will expect sex and he won't bother with foreplay because, as he actually tells her, "any woman looking at me gets turned on, so you're just lucky I chose you."

Jacob is an extreme case, but many of his behaviors are typical of the narcissistic man. He's obsessed with himself and with how others perceive him. He tries to control everything that might affect those perceptions. If you know a man like Jacob, or are married to him, run! He's not capable of change.

The Victim

The victim grew up in a dysfunctional family. He learned that the only way to get his needs met is by being extremely self-sufficient, stealthy and manipulative. A victim is clueless when it comes to relationships. He never learned nurturing skills because no one ever nurtured him. He invents his own truth to make himself look good and uses seduction in an attempt to find the missing elements in his life.

The victim learned his role by being neglected or by watching a parent being abused, either by the other parent or by another family member. Having witnessed this, he vacillates between being the victim and the abuser. Watching a seemingly weak parent who is struggling to navigate a system where another person appears to have all the power taught him how to act insignificant and helpless. Helplessness breeds self-pity; thus he blames others for everything that happens, refuses to take responsibility and makes excuses for every event. The paradox of a victim's irresponsibility is the gamut of feelings from failure to rage, guilt and shame, that run his life.

The victim never forgets a slight, brings up the same incident year after year, and wants an apology every time. He complains loudly to anyone who will listen and has few personal boundaries. He seeks sympathy. He sees himself mistreated by the world, by friends, family members, employers and neighbors. He feels bad and it has to be someone's fault. He looks for injustice. He sets himself up to be a target for people who will take advantage of him so he can complain about it. If they do not take advantage of him, he imagines they do.

Ask a victim what he is up to and he will tell you how he's been hurt, insulted, snubbed or in some way affronted. He thinks that he's performed well and his performance has gone unrecognized. He complains about his wife/girlfriend, complains about his boss, complains about his neighbors, does work for which he never is paid, and loans money he never gets back. Some big-hearted people fall for the victim's tales and try to help. Big mistake! He does not want help. He wants sympathy.

As a child, the victim was helpless to prevent the cruelty that happened to him and around him. He was simultaneously powerful and powerless: powerless because he could not stop what was going on around him, but powerful because he blamed himself for what was happening. He watched the underdog in his family get all the sympathy and all the attention. So he presents himself as the underdog in order to get love.

To preserve his power he uses financial deprivation, foul and offensive words, emotional blackmail, fists or blunt objects, and he can be a ticking time bomb. He wants you and everyone he knows to fill up the empty hole that is inside of him. His ego covers up a forlorn and pathetic person. Sensing this, you want to rescue him. You mistake your feelings of pity for love. You make excuses for his behavior and you tolerate his lack of consideration for you. You try to make things better by being understanding. You commiserate, console and sympathize to no avail. Eventually, you are fed up with his determination to be miserable. He will then turn to other people in his life—children, neighbors, relatives, even complete strangers—for solace.

If you want something from a person who is determined to remain a victim, forget it! The best thing you can do for a victim is call him on his behavior. Stop rescuing him. Stop making excuses for him. Tell him candidly how his behavior is affecting you, but do not expect thanks. He has the ability to take everything you say and turn it into an attack.

Loraine and Barry

When Loraine met Barry, she was instantly attracted to him. Not only did he have a great body, but also he seemed somewhat shy and kind of lost. When he smiled, her heart did a happy dance. She made the first move by inviting him to meet her at a party. He came and looked strikingly handsome in his silk shirt and linen slacks. She could tell right away that he was ill at ease so she did everything in her power to make him feel comfortable, going out of her way to introduce him to friends and be a sparkling companion. She complimented him on the things she liked about him every chance she got.

When he called the next day and invited her out she excitedly agreed. Their first kiss sent her to heights of passion that she hadn't experienced for a long time. During the next few months, Loraine listened politely to his stories of exploitation and mistreatment by his first wife, by his boss, by his family, and by his friends. It seemed they had all used him or neglected him or taken advantage of him. Barry told his stories with such conviction and such sincerity that it didn't even occur to Loraine to question their validity. She saw that he was always busy doing things for a lot of people—including her.

When Loraine discovered that Barry was also telling stories about her, and found out that he deeply resented many of things he did for her, she was devastated and sought help. It was then she realized that she was in a relationship with a classic victim who made getting people to feel sorry for him his life's work.

Loraine found that Barry could say mean, insulting things to her when there was no one around, and that he could easily take everything she did or said and turn it into an assault on himself. Why does she stay? Because she "loves" him and because she hopes that one day, he will wake up to the truth that he is making himself miserable. Loraine tells me there is a limit to her forbearance but she hasn't reached it yet.

Every woman in a relationship with a victim needs to take a good look at herself and her penchant for rescuing people. This is a great opportunity for her to learn how to set limits, how not to fall prey to the victim's poor me stories, and when to detach. She must stop trying to "help" him and work on her own issues, which include being an easy mark for a hard-luck story.

The Little Boy

The little boy has a honey-tongued charm that attracts the mother in a woman. If I have heard it once, I have heard it a thousand times: "He's my third (fourth, fifth) child." You say it with resignation and annoyance in your voice. You love a man who is willing to let you take the reins and make the rules, and in so doing, you took your man to raise.

When you tell a man how to dress and how to think, when you tell him to "get out of the way" and let you do something, when you wait on him, pick up after him, and do things for him that he should be doing for himself, this is an affront to his maturity. When you pay his bills, fix his lunch, let him drive your car, let him always sleep at your house (if you're single) or make the rules for the household, you are acting as his mother. Acting as a guy's mother is a double-edged sword. On the one hand, you like the power; on the other hand, you are exhausted. You saw his child-like behavior when you were dating and you found it appealing. You thought he would grow up once the two of you became a committed couple. He's caught in a double bind as you signal that you both love and hate his childishness. His real mother was abusive, absent, or neglectful and gave him the same message.

You were born to be motherly, so of course he found you. He turned to you for advice, consolation and reassurance. You could not be more willing to provide assistance, so you call him, because he is too busy to call you. A dozen times a day you text him just to make sure he knows you care. You remind him of appointments. You make sure you are available when he needs you. You make the social arrangements. You wait on him and serve him food. You take time off from work to help him with a project. You give him gifts and plan special surprises for him. He rarely does the same for you. Your feelings are hurt but you keep on giving, hoping that he will take a clue from your generosity. It makes you feel good to be helpful. It makes him irresponsible.

Perhaps you are trying to help him in an attempt to make up to him what he did not receive in childhood or past relationships. Many men have learned, because we have taught them, that a story involving an abusive childhood or a former odious wife will get them the nurturing they so desperately need and are afraid to ask for. It is important to understand that neither you nor any other woman can ever make restitution to a man for what happened to him in the past. Forget it. It is his job to heal his past. You can, however, support him in seeking help.

When you mother your partner, you create a covertly incestuous relationship. Guys do not have (good) sex with their mothers. You have noticed that he is not all that great in bed, or he was, and now he seems to have lost interest. You are hoping it will get better. You try to talk to him about it but he seems disinterested. You wonder what's wrong. Is he gay? Asexual? Having sex elsewhere?

Some of you complain that your man gapes, ogles, and undresses other women with his eyes even while he is sitting or walking beside you. When confronted with this behavior he denies or refutes your observation. Or he says something like, "It's okay to look; I'm not touching her or doing anything wrong." He does not recognize that this little boy behavior is instilling a deep sense of inadequacy in you. He thinks he is just being a man. Someone (yes, you) must tell him that a grown-up man does not behave this way. I once dated a man for a short time who felt the need to make sexual comments and pull every woman, including waitresses, onto his lap. This is bad-mannered and unacceptable behavior on many levels. Do not tolerate it.

If you want a liberating, mature relationship, stop being the mother. If you do not know how to be an equal partner, join a women's group and listen to what other women expect from a mate. Recognize what you are doing and when you are doing it. Then change one behavior at a time.

Alice and Brian

Alice's husband Brian is a happy-go-lucky sort of guy and the kids love him because he's fun and he plays with them. Alice handles the money and pays the bills. She buys his clothes. She oozes concern as she nurtures him with back rubs and makes his lunch for work so he will eat the right things. She stays up late to finish up the housework or write out the checks for the bills while he goes to bed early to get his rest. She calls him at work just to tell him she loves him, and she is patient and understanding when he is wrapped up in activities that don't include her. They live in a house that has had a broken picture window for fifteen years and kitchen cupboards without doors on them, which he intends to fix someday.

He holds a full time job with much responsibility but doesn't do much of anything at home, which astonishes Alice. It seems Brian's mom didn't expect much from him and his dad made a career of sitting in his recliner. Brian won't take responsibility unless she nags him, and then he can't do it well enough for her. When he speaks, she corrects him; when he gets dressed, she tells him what to wear. She encourages him to see the doctor and the dentist and makes sure there is enough money to pay for the visits. If he doesn't feel like going to work, she calls in sick for him.

Alice grew up having to raise her siblings because her father was absent and her mother was working all the time—and needed her. She is a natural mother. She takes charge without thinking about it and she doesn't demand much in return. At this point Alice is keeping Brian around because the children love him. They've never had a mutually satisfying relationship and they never will. Their only hope is for her to learn to sit on her hands and keep her mouth shut. If she does this, he might decide to grow up. But she can't do this until she recognizes that she likes being the mother. It gives her a sense of satisfaction and it's the only kind of love she's ever known.

The Addict

The addict lives for alcohol, drugs, work, sex, food or other compulsive behaviors. His addiction is the major focus of his life. Addiction is an illness, and you don't have a prayer of taking its place as the center of his affections. The important thing is not what he is addicted to, but how this addiction behaves. He is rarely or never there for you. His drinking, his buddies, his job, they come first. Always, with addiction, there is the abuse of neglect, sometimes accompanied by violence. The addict is often missing when something important is going on in the family. He spends money he does not have, or money you need for things that are more important. Or, if his addiction is money, he deprives you of basic needs and is stingy to the core. He has many difficulties with life and can never quite get it together.

If you are dealing with addiction, you need more information than this book can give you. Please, please, know that you are a valuable, worthwhile human being and go get the help and information you need to deal with the addict. A saying in Al-anon is, "if you don't like being a doormat, then get off the floor."

Elaine and Bruce

They both drank a lot and smoked a little pot now and then. It used to be they would only do it on vacation or for a special occasion. Then Bruce started drinking after work with some of his sales associates. At first he always made it home in time for dinner, then he started calling Elaine to tell her he would be home "in a little bit." Sometimes she fed the kids dinner and waited for him to show up so she could eat with him. Then he stopped calling and started coming home late in the evening, then the middle of the night and finally sometimes not until the next day.

Elaine is furious with him. She doesn't understand why he can't have a couple of drinks and then quit for the night. She has started driving around looking for him, and sometimes she sends the kids into the bar to get him to come out. She paces the floor and worries constantly that he's been in an accident. Or that maybe he is out with another woman. For a while, she tried stocking the refrigerator with beer, thinking that would keep him home. Then she tried joining him at the bar and drinking with him. She is convinced that he doesn't love her because if he did, he would be home with her and the kids.

His mood swings baffle her. Sometimes, when he's sober, he is sweet and contrite and can't do enough to please her, and sometimes, when he's drunk, he is loud and abusive. She makes excuses for his behavior and blames his friends, his boss and even his mother (who clearly didn't raise him right). She does everything she can to protect him, trying hard to control how much he drinks, and nothing works. She secretly thinks he drinks because there is something wrong with her. She doesn't understand that alcoholism is a progressive disease that can't be controlled even by the person who has it. Elaine would do well to search out the nearest Al-anon meeting and start attending regularly. When I suggested this, her first words were, "I can't do that. What would people think?" If she would take this suggestion, she would be amazed at the people she finds there that she knows—wives of lawyers and judges, wives of ministers and doctors, mothers of famous athletes and possibly her next-door neighbor. If she gives Al-anon a chance, her life will change in some amazing ways. If she doesn't, it is because her pride is more important that her relationship.

Chapter 5

The kind of love no woman wants

Just yesterday I was talking with a woman who was in tears because her daughter is married to an abusive man. He screams at her, tears her down, makes fun of her and pushes her around.

"I can't get her to leave him," she said.

"Where did she learn this behavior?" I asked.

"Well," she said, "I suppose it was from watching me and her step-father fight. He was really mean to her."

Women who are abused often do not know it is abuse. I know this sounds ridiculous, but when a woman grows up in a family where hitting, screaming, silent treatment, threats, neglect and other types of mistreatment are normal and regular occurrences, she has a difficult time labeling the behavior as abuse. She does not like it and it hurts. She puts all her energy into trying to make him stop, because she blames herself for what is happening.

An abused woman endures inhuman treatment for several reasons:

- Her false pride won't let her admit she needs help;
- She thinks she is doing something to cause the abuse;
- She believes she has nowhere to go;
- She is in denial about the severity of the problem; or
- She thinks she can get him to change.

Many women have a savior complex. They actively, albeit unconsciously, search for people to save and for those needing care. Why? Because they learned to be caretakers at a young age. Someone in their family expected them to take undue responsibility for other members in the family. Often as little girls they were forced to raise siblings, and they received much needed love for doing this. Now they only feel worthwhile if they are rescuing or orchestrating the lives of others—who often abuse them in the process.

"Savior complex" is a psychological term used to describe people who feel noble when they give away time, advice, money and energy to help people who should be helping themselves. Some people call this behavior codependent. Codependency is a survivor skill, learned at an early age, and it may one day be the death of the person who has it. My working definition of a codependent is this: living a life you hate to keep the peace, and giving up your self to keep from being abandoned.

If you fit this mold then your sympathetic personality attracts victims and abusers. You try to take care of your need for love by taking care of others. Codependents, as well as abusers, are empty people. When two empty people connect and try to have a relationship, this causes chaos, confusion and huge disappointment. The emptiness only grows larger. You find yourself swimming upstream all the time. You find yourself saying things like, "I do everything for everybody and nobody does anything for me." You struggle with your health and your level of exhaustion. You work overtime for no pay. The school calls you for help with activities. You continually try harder to make sense of things or to make relationships work. You are the thoughtful one, the compassionate one, but recognize that you are also the one who helps people shirk responsibility. Everyone leans on you and expects you to be there for them. You took your mother's advice to heart when she said, "Do unto others as you would have them do unto you," but you missed what James Dobson said his in book *Tough Love*: "no reciprocity, no dice."

Love is not supposed to hurt. If you are being threatened, cussed at, spoken to with contempt or faced with a partner's rage, you must seek help. It is not your fault. You cannot make someone behave abusively. You are not the cause of his contempt, his sarcasm, his rage or his poor self-esteem. He blames you so he won't have to look at himself.

Love him if you must, but then let him go and move on. You can love a man without having to have him. You deserve love from someone who is emotionally healthy. Do not waste your time praying and hoping that he will change or come around someday. Wish him well and go find yourself a man with integrity. One who is responsible, accountable, dependable, generous and able to give as good as he gets. It is important to learn to hold your ground calmly, speak your truth and hold yourself accountable for your contribution to the problem. If this puts you in danger, learning to state your needs must be secondary to developing a plan for safety.

Nora and Ken

Nora and Ken started dating when they were sophomores in high school. She was brunette, petite and pretty, and had gorgeous, creamy skin. He was an athlete with a great body and lots of blond curly hair. She helped him with his homework. He walked her home from school every day and made sure she never had a dateless Saturday night. They comforted each other when things got bad at their respective homes. Ken's step-mother could be a real bitch and Nora's truck driver dad was often gone.

As soon as they graduated from high school, they found an apartment and moved in together. Both got jobs and everything looked great from the outside. Nora never told anyone that Ken shoved her onto the bed on their first night together and demanded to know what she was "laughing about with the guy who brought the furniture." She was devastated but excused him because this was a big step and he was anxious about it. It wasn't the first time he'd mistreated her. There had been many times during high school when he'd blown up at her. On prom night, they'd had to leave early because she'd been having "too much fun." He had stopped the car at her house and shoved her out the door, calling her "a slut." The next day he'd brought her flowers and begged her to forgive him. He was always sorry.

She came to my attention when a minister gave her my phone number. It seems they were out on Saturday night and both had had a little too much to drink. Ken went from a jolly, good time guy to one who manhandled Nora when he locked the car door and beat on her in the parking lot. People tried to intercede but they couldn't get the door open. By the time the police arrived, Ken and Nora were already home and Nora was putting ice on her bruises.

If you know a woman who is being abused and she hangs in there for more abuse, tell her you know what is happening. Do not insist that she leave. Insist, instead, that she is a valuable worthwhile woman; tell her everything good about herself that you can think of to say, and tell her often. She is not hearing it at home and the only way she can leave is to get her self-esteem back. Keep informing her of her value; keep reminding her that she is a person to be cherished. Keep telling her that she deserves better treatment. Tell her to fight for what she wants—and that you will help her do it. And, most importantly, if she is in danger, help her to make a plan for safety.

CHAPTER 6

Jealousy leaves everyone wanting

Jealousy is about fear of loss, lack of trust and a belief in the scarcity principle. People do strange things if they believe that there is only so much love in the world and one must fight for a share. Jealousy is called "the green-eyed monster," and it disrupts the lives of many people, both male and female. I have witnessed bloody barroom brawls caused by jealousy. I have watched church women destroy each other over who gets to make decisions about ultimately unimportant issues. I have worked in offices where one employee deliberately sabotages another to earn the boss's favor. I have also been the target of jealousy numerous times, personally and professionally. I have experienced mean-spirited gossip and sabotage. It hurts the most when it comes from a significant other or someone you think is a friend. The lower a person's sense of self-worth, the more likely jealousy will occur. Jealous people cause heartache and destruction wherever they go. You can accept them, love them unconditionally and reassure them, but this is never enough.

Joe and Ginny

Joe and Ginny sit in my office glaring at each other. They have not been married very long.

"He follows me to work and waits outside of my job to follow me home after work," she says. "He calls me three or four times a day and if I don't answer, he gives me the third degree when I get home at night. He checks my cell phone for calls. He's constantly saying, 'Where were you? What were you doing?' And I'm sick of it."

He says, "I don't trust her. She lies about what she is doing."

"I do not!" she yells with tears in her eyes.

"Oh yeah, last week I called and called your cell and you didn't answer. Then, when you got home, you had a bag of stuff from the store. Who did you meet at the store? And who is that guy you said hi to when we went out to eat? How do you know him?"

This conversation goes back and forth for forty minutes while she explains each incident away.

Finally, he explodes with the truth. "My first wife was messing around with my best friend right under my nose. That will never happen to me again."

When I suggest to him that he has some work to do on this issue he says, "I'm not doing anything until she gets her act together."

While Ginny is frustrated with Joe, she is also somewhat pleased. She thinks his jealousy is because he loves her so much. Jealousy does not prove love; it proves a lack of personal self-esteem, a need to control and, of course, fear, none of which has anything to do with love. Unfortunately, Ginny is giving up work opportunities, family and friends just to keep the peace. Jealousy holds her hostage. Joe's close watchfulness is creating the very thing he fears. He will lose her if he continues in this vein.

To save her sanity, she must learn not take his behavior personally. She must learn not to react to his assumption or waste time protesting her innocence. His fear—and his behavior—belong to him and it's not about her; in fact, it doesn't have anything to do with her. She doesn't have enough power to make him behave badly.

She must reach out to her family and her friends; unfortunately, they don't live nearby. I encouraged her to tell them anyway and to reach out to other women at work. She must not keep his behavior a secret.

If you are in a relationship with a jealous mate then you most likely walk on eggshells much of the time. Chances are you have developed a fear of relating to others and have given up some activities that are meaningful for you. Maybe you have even stopped saying "hi" or hugging an acquaintance when your mate is around. You are doing this to keep the peace.

You can't do anything about another person's conduct beyond refusing to allow it to define you. His insecurity is based on false messages he gives himself. This person gives himself ideas that fit with his concept of who he is and, also, who you are. When he feels unworthy or insignificant, he tells himself he's inferior and you must be also or you wouldn't be with him. Therefore he can't trust you.

People who aren't trustworthy don't trust others. People who lie or cheat think that everyone is doing this. If you have checked your moral code and know that you are innocent of the accusations then know that whatever you are being accused of is true of the person doing the accusing. People without integrity won't expect to find it in you.

If you are in a relationship with a jealous man, don't apologize, explain or change your behavior. These are his demons and he has to fight them by himself. If you actually are morally or ethically wrong, clean up your act simply because you will like yourself better if you do. If you have been in this relationship for a long time, your vision of your worth may be skewed. Find a life coach or a counselor to help you sort out the truth.

Chapter 7

The media tells us what we want

The media, which is controlled by money, dictates what is glamorous and what is sexy. The media and the fashion world periodically change fashions and introduce new ideas in order to keep the money flowing. Public opinion is formed from media information and a woman who allows herself to be controlled by the media's portrayal of the "perfect woman" has an Achilles heel. Try as she might, she can never quite fit in because as soon as she acquires the new fashions and the new attitudes, they change. The media drives the need, not just to fit in, but to excel. Marketers study women's habits and their purchases in an effort to understand and exploit their insecurities. They do research on women's fears of:

- losing the man,
- losing the job,
- growing old,
- being alone and
- not being good enough (or pretty enough or thin enough or …)

Women represent billions of dollars to business, so businesses have a huge investment in making women feel badly about themselves. Marketers know that ugliness is a psychological issue and they bombard women with notice of fabricated imperfections.

Everything in the media is geared to make a woman feel like less of a person if she doesn't fall in line and "make herself better." Women are led to believe that face-lifts, breast enhancements, fanny lifts, liposuction, white teeth and the right weight will solve all of the problems they have with men. Years ago, companies marketed contact lenses with the slogan, "men seldom make passes at girls who wear glasses." Today Victoria's Secret hires beautiful, young, anorexic-looking models to parade down a runway in skimpy, lacy lingerie—wearing wings. The implication here is that if you buy their products you will become an angel and look like them.

Many fashion models choose between starving themselves and losing their source of income. A large number of women constantly fight to look like those glamorous, lanky models, even though they know the models are impossibly young—and filmed through an airbrushed lens. Women put themselves through many diets, surgeries and exercise programs. Some are doing it for the right reason, which is to enhance their health. Others are doing it to please someone else. A friend once told me she'd had breast reduction surgery because she thought her husband would be more attracted to her if she did this. Other friends have had all manner of surgical interventions to improve their looks. I too have gone through the nipping, tucking and pain of recovery because, unfortunately, beautiful people have more advantages in school, in the business world and in life in general. An impossible standard of beauty causes even beautiful teenage girls to have plastic surgery. Worse, their mothers are encouraging them because they want their daughters to be popular and successful.

Women read tons of self-help books in an effort to understand what is going on in their lives. Magazines that tell them *Fifty Ways To Satisfy A Man Sexually* and *Ten Things To Pique His Interest And Get Him To Call Back* fly off the shelves. Nearly every "woman's" magazine has a *Foolproof Diet!* splashed across the cover. These are placed strategically at the checkout counter in every store frequented by women.

Some women are disillusioned and tired of the game. A beautiful, forty-year-old friend is disenchanted with men and the rat race of hair, make-up, diets and sucking in her stomach. She hasn't been very successful with men, not because of her hair, her make-up or her body, but because she doesn't realize her own value. She doesn't grasp just how beautiful she is inside and out. So she hooks up with men to whom healthy women wouldn't give the time of day.

Women in their fifties often feel invisible because of our youth-loving culture. They must develop a core of self-assurance and confidence in their abilities. These women have sexual powers, intelligence and poise that can only be assumed by living through many obstacles and difficulties. Never sell yourself short or take a back seat to anyone. Never let age determine how beautiful or sexy you feel.

We must learn not to let the media dictate the standards for beauty and desirability. One thing we can all do is boycott the magazine industry that insists on exploiting our desire to be loved and appreciated. We can stop buying publications that feature teen-age anorexic models.

Stop believing the fallacy that your worth depends on your looks and the clothes you wear. Who are you? What do you like about yourself? Know that there are people out there who love you just the way you are, and you too can decide to love yourself just the way you are. Take a leaf from the book of the less than perfect-looking women who have made it big in movies and TV. They made it because they believed in themselves—and you can too.

CHAPTER 8

The woman who wants more and better sex

A woman can deepen, increase, compound and intensify her sex life with the right sexual viewpoint. Unfortunately, some of us have unhealthy attitudes, and some of us are just plain uninformed concerning the intricacies of sex. The "sex talks" in schools are usually dry facts about eggs and sperm, fallopian tubes, seeds and plumbing. The sex talks at home, for most girls, include the word "don't," and many aren't informed about herpes, AIDs and sexually transmitted infections. It is the rare woman who grows up in a home where she learns the complexities of sex along with the value of her person. This subject is difficult for most parents to address, and kids of all genders are often expected to learn it through the schools—or by osmosis. Television and movies give totally unrealistic impressions of love, lust and passion. Soap operas glamorize sex to the point of ruining the real thing for a lot of women.

Down through the ages men have believed that women should be subject to male sexual desires. Women were taught to suppress sexual feelings, which wasn't all that hard to do because many men were inexperienced and selfish lovers. We are more enlightened now, but women are still confused about their right to go after the hot-blooded hankering that burns in their loins. Women are passionate creatures. Passion is a powerful emotion and a driving force for an exhilarating sexual experience. Lust is part of the chemistry that nature provides to guarantee procreation. Love doesn't necessarily need to be present for lust and passion to exist. This is something every man knows and few women accept.

When the sex in a relationship is good, it is no more important than any other facet of a well-balanced relationship. If it is bad, it becomes monumental. In some relationships, sex is basically nonexistent because the parties gave up trying or because sex with someone who doesn't satisfy emotional needs is basically an exercise in futility.

Shana came to see me, furious and discouraged with her sex life. She said she could hardly stand to sleep in the same bed with her husband, because he ignored her and went to sleep with his back to her. In her words, she was "horny all the time." But when they did have sex, his "slam, bam, thank you, ma'am" style left her angry and full of a craving that wasn't being satisfied. In addition to this, he frequently spent evenings submerged in his computer or the TV, and then expected to hop into bed, get it on, roll over and go to sleep. Shana's question was, "What am I doing wrong? What is wrong with me?"

The first thing we worked on was her willingness to take all the blame for her discontent. "Maybe it's my weight," she said. "Maybe I am just not interesting enough, or pretty enough or sexy enough." It took a few sessions to get her to understand that these might be the excuses she was giving herself, but they actually had nothing to do with the crux of the problem. The reality: she was hampered by shame, fear and ignorance concerning sex. She was afraid to discuss this with her husband. When she tried to talk with him about it, she became tongue-tied and stammered, and he suddenly got very busy and brushed her off.

The other reality is that he didn't know any better. There is a myth about sex, the myth that a real man is always hot to trot and women are reserved and non-responsive. Nothing could be further from the truth. The complaints I hear from women are often the opposite of this. If there is a sexual problem in the relationship, it is not actually about intercourse but about attitudes, insecurity, hidden resentments and expectations.

There is no need to have a paltry or insignificant sex life, and there is no shame in wanting a terrific sexual experience. I gave Shana an instructional videotape to walk her through the intricacies of good sex. I also gave her a good book, (The Tao of Love and Sex by Jolan Chang). I invited her read the book alone or to share it with her husband. She was afraid he would judge her harshly, and opted to do these things in secret. Did it work? Only to a point. But at least it took the cork out of the bottle. She is enlightened now about the way others view sex, and she now knows that she is not the cause of her husband's behavior. As Shana refuses to participate in non-verbal, careless love-making and is learning to say what she wants, her husband is slowly responding. Who knows what kind of demons concerning sex are running around in his head? She doesn't, because he won't say anything other than, "It's just a subject we never talked about at home."

Most everyone wants good sex. It gives a feeling of well-being unlike any other. Unfortunately, sex is a sensitive subject and often difficult to discuss. If your sex life is not meeting your needs, you must find a way to share this fact with your partner. What you share must be without blame or castigation, which is sometimes hard for people who have been nursing resentments for a long time. So first get rid of the resentments. You can do this by talking with a professional person who can help you work through your feelings, or you can do it by journaling and writing down everything you feel. Not everything you think. Thoughts are not facts, but people often think they are. Feelings, on the other hand, cannot be disputed.

You have a right to ask for and enjoy good sex. If this is not happening, you have a decision to make, either to tolerate the lack of sexual fulfillment in your relationship or to make an issue of it. I know women who love their mates but have sex with someone outside the relationship. I don't recommend this.

Julie and Matt

Julie and Matt came to talk to me about the constant misunderstandings that were wrecking their "happy home." We discussed communication skills, relationship techniques and many bones of contention. The subject of sex came up, but Matt didn't want to talk about it, even though Julie had revealed that she asks him for oral sex and more romance, but he was turned off by this request. About six months into our counseling sessions, Julie revealed to me that she was having an affair. Her dishonesty was eating her alive. She was hoping that she could get her marriage on track and just sort of slink away from the affair with no one the wiser. I suggested that she level with her husband. She wouldn't, because they were in the middle of buying a new house and they had two little children. She was afraid he would dump her and take the kids and the house. She excused the affair because of their dismal sex life. Her husband only knew one move: stick it in, move it around, and flop exhausted on top of her when it was over. Her lover on the other hand had all kinds of moves, rented nice motel rooms, filled them with flowers, brought her exotic foods and said all the romantic things her heart longed to hear. Knowing about Julie's affair and her refusal to tell Matt, I could not continue to work with them as a couple, so I told them that because the subject of sex couldn't be examined, they were finished with me. I urged her to stop the affair, but I don't know if she did or not.

Julie and Matt's problem manifested as a sex problem, but it actually was a problem of deep insecurity, poor sexual education and dangerous disregard for the sanctity of marriage. Julie must take total responsibility for having the affair. She does not get off the hook by saying that if Matt had been willing to meet her sexual needs, it probably wouldn't have happened. When there are secrets in a relationship, fear, resentments, betrayal and a refusal to move out of ignorance. These secrets destroy the glue that holds the fragile connection of two hearts together.

Can a man learn to get past his inability to hear from his mate concerning her needs without hearing them as a reflection of his own inadequacies in the sex department? Only if he is free from pride and arrogance and has a good measure of self-esteem. She must present her needs to him simply and honestly, without apology. He must be able to see it as a challenge and an opportunity for him to please her as well as himself.

For women who find themselves stammering, stuttering, and apologizing, know what you want to say. Practice saying it aloud until it feels natural and ordinary, then pick a time and just say it. What he does with what you say is his problem. As long as your material is presented without blame, you have done what you can do. The ball is in his court. If he doesn't want to play ball, what is your payoff for staying with him? Kids, money, houses and even health insurance are used as excuses, and these are sometimes valid, sometimes not. I know women who live with men and haven't had sex for months or even years. Women have told me that they have the "perfect brother-sister relationship," but they usually say this ruefully and with a shrug of their shoulders.

One woman I talked with recently said "my husband is not into sex. I choose to keep busy doing other things—working, politics, volunteer stuff and running ten miles a day—because he is so good to me in other ways." It's her life and her carefully considered choice. One must sometimes weigh the pros and cons and accept that there is no perfect man. There will always be something that you don't like about him. The question is, can you live with it?

Good sex can't be forced. If you want it, go to a sex therapist or sexual workshop (by yourself, if necessary). Be open and willing to listen and learn. Combat your fear and all your preconceived notions, and ditch your pride. A list of available sex therapists can be found through the American Association of Sexuality Educators, Counselors and Therapists (www.AASECT.org). Also, Dr. Ruth Westheimer, a noted sex educator and TV personality, has written thirty-five books on the subject of good sex. The information is available; you simply have to access it. If money is a problem, almost every community has a Planned Parenthood office. Go and ask for literature. There are also many free things on the internet that are informational and not pornographic. Stick with well-known experts such as Dr. Ruth.

Girls, young women and even some senior citizens that I know see sex with multiple partners as acceptable and justified because, after all, men have always done this. "So why can't I?" You can, but be sure you have the guts to insist on safe sex measures, HIV tests—and ask the herpes question. If a man refuses to wear a condom, do not let him touch you. This is true even if possible pregnancy is not an issue because, remember, you are having sex with everyone he's ever had sex with. He could be carrying a yeast infection or worse. Don't be fooled by his claims that condoms are uncomfortable and he's insulted that you would even ask. A beautiful eighteen-year-old girl with long dark hair and stunning blue eyes sat in my office crying because the guy she trusted gave her herpes. She now will have to tell every man she wants to have a relationship with that she has this debilitating disease and many will turn away from her.

Be sure you are having sex that is right for you and not going through the motions because of fear of abandonment. Be sure that you are not having sex as a way of manipulating him to do things for you. Above all, be sure that you are having sex with someone you can trust. For those of you who are still dating, don't jump into bed with a new guy until you have known him for a long time, respect yourself enough to wait at least three months or even longer.

Sometimes a person's illness or physical disability makes sex impossible or uncomfortable. Masturbation is an acceptable substitute for either partner.

However, do not use it to avoid intimacy or to avoid doing the hard work of developing a wholesome connection. Some people think that all affection and cuddling is a build-up to sex. This is faulty thinking. Good relationships set aside time to just cuddle, kiss and be together without this behavior always leading to sex. Start with hugs and snuggling and make it plain that this is as far as it goes—this time. This takes the pressure off both people and allows you just to enjoy the physical contact.

A healthy woman who doesn't want to have sex with her mate owes him an explanation even if that explanation is extremely uncomfortable for both of them. A person who is old enough to have a sexual relationship is old enough to learn how to talk about it. Buy a book or DVD and share it. If he doesn't want to participate in this, the problem is obviously his.

Sex is not for cowards. Go after what you want. Ask your man what moves turn him on. Ask him what he finds sexy. Ask him just to lay still and let you make love to him. The last time I said all of this to a client she said, "Yes, this all sounds good, but I can't stand him. He disgusts me." We worked to clear away the garbage in her mind concerning sex. In her case, there was childhood sexual abuse that had to be dealt with before she could have a good sexual experience. She started by being honest, first with herself and then with him. She never wanted him to know what had happened to her as a little girl for fear he would judge her. He was caring, compassionate and able to be patient and understanding once he discovered what the real problem was. Up until she leveled with him, he thought his sexual needs were "disgusting." Eventually their sex life turned into a satisfying experience for them both. They sort of dropped off my radar until, one day, I was driving down the street and she was in a car coming from the other direction. She honked and waved frantically and motioned for me to pull off to the side of the road. When I stopped she came running up to the car and said, "Come and look at what I have." I went back to her car and saw a beautiful baby girl about three months old. "Life," she said, "is wonderful beyond my wildest dreams."

Sometimes partners have been married or in a long term relationship for twenty, thirty or more years. How do they keep the sex from getting boring? Well, how do you keep eating from getting boring? First of all, you let yourself get hungry. (Try cuddling, snuggling, touching, rubbing and kissing—but no intercourse.) Then you experiment with new recipes, you try out new spices and test new ideas. If what you are eating is boring and mundane, you don't blame the food, retire the stove or throw out the dishes; you make changes in your approach. You remember that a steady diet of anything gets boring after a while, so sometimes you eat a quick hot dog and other times you develop a seven course meal. You cultivate methods to make the food exciting and pleasing to your palette. This takes work and patience. It takes a sense of humor, and both must be willing to experiment. Buy some sex toys, play some make-believe games, have sex in your car or under the stars, introduce some mystery, develop some new fantasies or go to Esalen, a retreat center where people sit in hot-tubs and on the beach naked. Go on a trip, even if it is only a couple miles from home. Indulge in couples' massages.

"Yeah, he won't cooperate. He says he's too old and tired." All I can say to you is you have a right to a fulfilling life.

A sexually satisfied couple is easy to spot. I know a couple who have been together for a long time, and even in public they are constantly touching each other. They smile a lot. They have a mutual glow, a meeting of the eyes, a sense of energy, vitality and sizzle. He never misses a chance to say something good about her, and she rewards him with a "we have a secret" smile. I love being around them.

Don't ever forget that sex starts in the brain. The brain puts out what you put into it. Keep positive sexual thoughts about your mate uppermost in your mind daily. Put in negative thoughts about your body, cynical thoughts about your partner, stir in the lack of healthy information concerning desire and sex will be a chore. Put in positive, loving thoughts and sex can be exciting again. A good book to read on this subject is *The Return of Desire* by noted sex therapist Gina Ogden, Ph.D. She also does relationship workshops.

CHAPTER 9

A woman with class gets what she wants

Attitudes change, opportunities change, but the demeanor of a classy woman doesn't change. Class has a special distinction that is unmistakably graceful and diplomatic. I don't know who coined the term "trashy women," but I know that this term defines a behavior that polite society finds unacceptable. Some of you rebel at this and think the rules are outdated—think Madonna, Lady Gaga and Miley Cyrus. However, self-esteem and self-respect never go out of style. Rich does not replace class.

Class sets you apart from the pack and gives you an advantage in all areas of life. As a classy woman, you:

- Value yourself and your contribution to the world;
- Know that you're defined by your behavior;
- Have a spirit of generosity that goes beyond material things and expands to respectful encouragement of those you meet;
- Show up when someone you care about needs you;
- Take responsibility for your own behavior and apologize when necessary;
- Dress tastefully and in a manner befitting the femme fatale you know yourself to be inside;

- Know that sexiness is a measure of attitude, not the flaunting of T& A;
- Are honest and trustworthy;
- Stand up for your beliefs with dignity, while respectfully allowing others to have their own opinions;
- Don't indulge in gossip or negative chatter;
- Don't make vulgar comments or use four letter words;
- Have a sense of humor and can laugh at yourself;
- Do things for people who can never repay you;
- Ask courteously and assertively for what you want, expecting to get it; and
- Focus on the good in your world.

Do not mistake a woman's quiet acquiescence or submission to the status quo for class. Women like Maya Angelou, Barbara Walters, Elisabeth Hasselbeck, Taylor Swift and Michelle Obama are all the epitome of class. They have a certain elegance of style, taste and manners. They have causes, principles, determination and are outspoken about beliefs. I see them claiming their feminine power and exhibiting intelligence, compassion, graciousness, sassiness and strength. They have met the challenge of tradition and used it to construct a world in which they excel in spite of the obstacles.

I am friends with a woman who oozes class. I have never heard her use a four letter word. I have never experienced her engaging in gossip. I have watched her battle illness, loneliness, and negative public opinion. She expresses strong sentiments in a way that allows others to disagree with her if they so choose. She quietly does things for other people that no one knows about. I have heard her express her strengths in a way that is not bragging but admits she has some special talents. She is ageless, somewhere in mid-life, and she is quietly proud of her sexual powers. She doesn't question what happened in her life; she celebrates it, the bad as well as the good. She is strong, encouraging and always ready with a kind word.

For more information about what constitutes class, see Chapter 14 in the Men's Section of this book.

CHAPTER 10

A real problem in getting what you want

In many years of dealing with you, I have heard a large number of bad man stories. However, the worst stories I hear are those about how we treat each other. Mothers are jealous of daughters. Sisters fight. Co-workers step on each other's necks to get the promotion or the favor of the male boss. Friends gossip about each other. Women with important positions in business often do everything they can to keep other women from making it to the top.

Stories of peer bullying and abuse that start in grade school go on ad infinitum. I have heard many accounts of jealousy, snobbery, name calling, gossip, snubs, rejection and deliberate ridicule. Ten-year-old girls tell me they hide in the bathroom at school because they are not wearing the right brand of clothing.

Unenlightened women are at war, the war of winning men's favor. It is a war of scarcity; a war of power and, worse, a war of personal victory at the expense of other women. We must stop this behavior.

Women with integrity do not trash other women, date their best friend's mate or boyfriend, have affairs with another woman's husband or lie about a friend behind her back. The cyber-bullying that is now taking place among young girls and women, sometimes aided by their mothers, is a present tragedy and is downright sickening—but it is nothing new. Women have always vied for favor.

We must behave like women in combat, but not with each other. Instead, we must battle stereotypes, ignorance and fear. We must teach our daughters—and other young girls with whom we have contact—to treat each other with compassion and respect. We must know in our hearts that change starts with us. We can do it, in spite of others who may not yet be enlightened. There are enough jobs, enough men and enough opportunities for all of us if we simply work together.

Some say that Geraldine Ferraro lost her bid for vice-president because women rose up against her, women who demanded to know how she could raise a family and serve her country at the same time. Men called her pushy and she was asked if she knew how to bake blueberry muffins.[3] Has anyone ever asked a man this question? It's a harsh disappointment for a woman to lose a race because members of her own gender do not take pride in helping her reach her goal. How dare any of us hold another woman down because of our own gender biases and hypercritical attitudes?

Women must give each other the backing and encouragement needed to accomplish their goals. Years ago I desperately wanted to go to a month-long seminar about working with families. The cost was astronomical, but a female friend of mine cleaned out her savings account to make it possible for me to go. Her trust and belief in me gave me a hand up and a deep appreciation for her great desire to help. It took me a long time to pay her back but I did, and I had an undying gratitude for her.

Women often blame men for the lack of progress in their life ambitions. Nearly every woman has a story of a man who sabotaged her efforts in business or finances. Yet, there are also many stories of men who made women's advancement possible. In a woman's effort to have what she wants in life, she must realize that men are not the enemy. There are many smarter than average men who love women and know that giving a woman a hand up will bring them appreciation, recognition, acknowledgement and admiration. It is often fear and indifference on the part of other women that is the enemy. A woman who doesn't give another woman a hand up keeps her under the glass ceiling. She does it because of jealousy and her belief that another woman's success makes her look inadequate.

---

[3] *Newsweek*, September 22, 2008.

It is women who defeated the last woman running for president. Hillary Clinton's famous cookie remark outraged stay-at-home mothers. Why do women take other women to task for having ambition? This is Hillary's direct quote: "I could have stayed home and baked cookies and had teas, but what I decided to do was fulfill my profession."[4] Women, be aware that taking remarks like Hillary's personally will be your undoing. Have you ever heard a male politician say, "I could have gone into construction," and heard of construction workers causing an uproar because he said this? Doesn't every one of us have a right to fulfill our own destiny? Believe me: women outnumber men and if we wanted a woman president, we would have one. Women would make sure they are registered to vote, and they would vote for ambition and quality without allowing their husbands to tell them who to vote for. (You might think this doesn't happen, but it does.) This is not to say that women need to make decisions solely based on gender. Common sense, of course, must prevail.

Unfortunately, women are often suspicious and leery of each other. This lack of trust is a generational thing we must outgrow. This is a time when women can have it all just by supporting each other. There is no room for fear, judgment, envy or ridiculous attempts to keep other women from getting ahead. The best results occur when women seek out—and surround themselves with—other supportive women. If you are a woman who automatically assumes that men are smarter, more capable or more shrewd and discriminating, then study the history of powerful women who made your freedom to vote possible. Tough, stalwart and ingenious, they fought for our rights.

I have many loyal women friends who have gone out of their way to give me a hand up. I'm sorry to say I've also had a number of women in my life who were jealous and backbiting, some who slept with my former husband and some who almost destroyed my career. I forgive those women and pray for them. This allows me to move forward with my life, free of the baggage of bitterness and resentment. When we help and encourage other women to be emotionally and physically healthy, we're building a more secure foundation for our daughters and granddaughters. Don't hang out with a woman who criticizes you or a woman who constantly competes with you for the attention of a man. She is not your friend. A beloved colleague who is now deceased once said, "Men will pat your ass, but a woman will save it."

You are an amazing woman. If you want something, go after it. Don't listen to naysayers and critics. Make a written plan. Brainstorm, let your thinking go wild, and give yourself permission to dream. If something you want to do or be is very important to you, then take action. Don't threaten to do something or plan to do it someday. Do it now. There is no need to nag, pressure, or intimidate to get what you want. What you need to understand is that if something is important to you, it is important. If you can't do this on your own, get some professional help.

Don't let fear of change get in the way or give in to negative self-talk such as, "Maybe my mother is right. Maybe I am selfish." It is not selfish to take care of yourself. There is a huge difference between selfishness and self-preservation. Selfishness will lie, cheat and steal to get what it wants without regard to the needs of others. Self-preservation is knowing that what you want is vital to your happiness and calmly, without rancor, deciding you are worth it. You do not need to apologize or feel guilty for going after it.

Avoid negative people and negative attitudes and learn something new every day. Be grateful for the little things like a roof over your head, a bed to sleep on, food to eat, a delicious cup of coffee. Find and cultivate close women friends you can confide in, who will accept your imperfections with a sense of humor and do fun things with them. Buy sexy underwear and wear it smugly for yourself. Sleep naked. Seek spiritual experiences. Get a massage. Write poetry. Go sky diving, take a trip. Dream or meditate. Most of all, be true to yourself.

Each woman has an inner voice. Cultivate it and listen carefully to what it is saying. Learn how to communicate your wants and needs to the people who are important to you. Pick your battles. Do not engage in repeated arguments and useless oratory. Find the humor in your daily life and laugh out loud as often as possible. Seek women mentors and heroes. Be who and what you want to be and, above all, support other women in reaching for the moon.

SECTION TWO

For Men

WHO WANT TO KNOW
HOW TO PLEASE A WOMAN

CHAPTER 11

The woman who wants too much of you

Many a man has found himself in an intimate relationship with a controlling woman. Some unusual dynamics are in play when this happens. The attraction between them is based on uncompleted childhood nurture and training. She is driven by a manufactured image of herself that has come from being denied a self; to have a self a child must be invited to explore her world and encouraged to have her own thoughts and feelings. Raised by dominating, demanding parents who threatened abandonment whenever she tried to have an opinion, a desire or a feeling that did not meet their approval, or by parents who severely neglected her, she was forced to contrive an artificial self that would be pleasing to her parents and the outside world. She only knows life on a superficial level, and as long as she can control those around her, she does not have to look at the paradox of her dual personality—which is being extremely dependent and thinking herself completely self-reliant. In truth, she is both, and her greatest fear is that someone will see how worthless she is. Anyone who threatens her control threatens the very foundation of her existence.

Often this woman develops an addiction to food, work, prescription drugs or alcohol because it is a huge and exhausting endeavor to continually maintain control over all the people around her. She doesn't quibble or pay attention to your irrelevant objections to her plans and ideas. There is usually no discussion, so those who disagree with her are banished from her—and your—life.

The controlling woman presents as an authentic, fun, loving, talented and caring person. She learned long ago that this is what people (i.e., her parents) want to see in her, and she has learned her part well. She has denied her authentic self for so long that her façade almost feels real, yet she is constantly nagged by the reprehensible knowledge that she is a fake. She is a member of a secret society of counterfeit women who must manage, organize, manipulate and monitor all that goes on around them. She is not wholly to blame and, in truth, doesn't even know there is anything wrong with what she is doing. She is only doing what she has always done. Her defense is to put down, ridicule and criticize in order to keep her power, usually while smiling and flattering the people she can use to accomplish her ends. If she has a spouse or children, she keeps them subservient and compliant by threatening abandonment.

The man who finds himself in a relationship with her is attracted by her strength, her little girl wiles, her ability to discern and say what he most needs to hear and her seeming capacity to have fun. He is, in the beginning, thrilled and grateful that she seems to understand and desire him. If he is honest with himself, he is most attracted by her intensity and how secure it makes him feel.

Once he is dedicated to the relationship and she knows he is committed, the gloves come off and he suddenly finds that anything he does or says is not quite good enough. She always knows more or has a better way. She methodically and coldly works to sever his relationships with family and friends. In her mind these interlopers serve no purpose, and people are much easier to control if there are few outside influences. His attempts to make her happy will miss the mark because she has an idea in her head of how he should be—and he can never quite live up to it. So he tries harder and finds himself starting to feel hurt, angry and discouraged. Aware of her ability to shame and ridicule people, he dodges any thoughts of confrontation and soon finds himself reduced to a childlike status, being told what to do and think. To keep the peace, he abdicates responsibility and thus sets up an unequal balance of power. She now knows what she has always known: that she must do everything herself. No one is as capable as she is and she cannot rely on anyone.

She starts to blame him for everything that goes wrong and feels justified in doing so. As he bows to her determination to have things her way and to her seeming efficiency, he becomes more and more dependent on her and more fearful of abandonment. He takes his frustration and anger out on other people. He often tries to force them to please her too, and denounces himself as inadequate, covering up his hurt with trance-like amiability and becoming accident prone in the process.

She is rigid in her determination as insanity grips the household. Both are caught up in the paradoxical dynamic of selfless self-absorption. Without help, neither will understand that both are playing out a script handed to them in childhood by the parents they are emulating. As the relationship progresses, lack of accountability becomes a way of life for him. Her lack of respect and concern for his well-being will drive him to desperation. He will lie for her, cheat for her and steal for her, but in the end nothing will ever be enough because it was never about him in the first place. The more he rolls over, the less respect she will feel for him. She becomes even more controlling. She wants him to stand up to her and when he does, she smacks him down with discrediting remarks or gives him the silent treatment.

Nice guys get a lot of mileage out of being in relationships with controlling women. It makes them look decent, helpful, patient and kind. They have a splash of bad boy charm, and approach life in an immature adolescent way. They develop a victim mentality and a passive aggressive approach to conflict.

What the controlling woman wants is to feel safe and cared for by a man who stands up for himself with honesty, integrity and self-respect, a man who is compassionately impervious to her tears, threats, tantrums and threats of abandonment. The inconsistency is that once she finds this man, she will come face to face with her complete and total emptiness, which may frighten her so much she will quickly throw herself into the arms of the first controllable man she finds. Alternatively, she may nurture her addiction to work, food or drugs to avoid the painful glimpse of the barrenness that is her soul.

Until this woman does the hard work of finding her "self," no one can give her what she wants.

Chapter 12

Women! You can't live with them, and you can't live without them.

This expression has been repeated since the beginning of time. It's a statement of frustration. In your eyes, you are coffee and we are cream. In our eyes, we are fruit and you are nuts—and sometimes you're a marshmallow. Often the mystery of why we think differently from you about the same things poses a huge problem for you. Our thought process puzzles you. In much the same way, we find ourselves perplexed and frequently baffled by the things you say and the things you leave undone. To us, you are as fascinating as you are frustrating. Time and again, we are amazed by the choices you make.

In the 1964 movie *My Fair Lady*, Rex Harrison's Professor Henry Higgins sings the words, "Why can't a woman be more like a man?" about Audrey Hepburn's Eliza Doolittle. He's actually asking, "Why can't a woman recognize my superiority?" His enormous irritation with her femininity hides his inability to be who he really is—a man whose self-esteem is based entirely in his superiority. He's a successful man who lives completely in his head and considers women to be easily manipulated and controlled. She proves him wrong, and this drives him crazy.

Do you have a woman in your life who's driving you crazy?

As a counselor, I receive a huge blessing because men pay to talk with me. I get to see an image of you that many women would love to experience. I hear deep dark secrets, insecurities, dreams, ambitions and intimate details about your sex life. This does not make me an expert on men, it makes me a woman who respects and appreciates your efforts and your vulnerabilities. Some of you have been married for a while, some are single and cohabitating and some are single and live alone.

You need to be listened to when you are experiencing a dilemma and have exhausted all other possibilities for a resolution. When you come to my office, you are often apologetic and nervous because you never thought you would find yourself in a situation like this. You express anger, disbelief, confusion and guilt. Most often, you see yourself as inadequate and you are embarrassed that you can't solve your own problems.

You are a good man and you don't always know it. So you ask, "What makes her act the way she does?" You are relieved to hear that you are not alone. Many men face the same challenges.

Some of the issues men have shared with me are:

- "Why does she say she loves me and then go out with her old boyfriend?"
- "Why does she call her ex-husband to fix her car, when I'd gladly do it?"
- "Why does she go out with her friends and then wakes me out of a sound sleep, f-----g drunk and horny?"
- "Why does she tell me I am just like her father? I know he wasn't all that nice."
- "Why does she get this mad look on her face all the time and won't tell me what's wrong?"
- "Why isn't anything ever good enough for her?"
- "Why does she put the kids and her job first and all I get are leftovers?"
- "Why won't she clean the house and do the dishes?"
- "Why can't she empty the dishwasher?"
- "Why does she answer for me when someone asks me a question? She answers before I can even think about it."

WOMEN: WHAT DO WE WANT? • 61

- "Why does she wait until I am ready to go to bed to talk about money? We can sit and watch TV all night, and just when I want to give it up for the day, she brings up the bills."
- "Why does she say, 'Are you really going to wear that?' Is it wrong to want to be comfortable?"
- "Why does it bother her so much to see me relax? If I am lying on the couch or sitting in my recliner, she says something mean or gives me a chore to do."
- "Why does she get huffy when I don't want the same things she wants?"
- "Why does she spend the whole evening on the phone? If her friends aren't calling her, then she's calling them."
- "How can I get her away from that computer? She's constantly on it even while watching TV."
- "Why is she so disappointed in me? When I see that look on her face, I get pissed."

These questions are screaming for answers, so let's examine your expectations. What do you want from her?

- Do you, like Freud, want your women to be simple and reasonable?
- Do you work hard to understand her?
- Do you try to manhandle her?
- Do you give her what she wants and then make her pay in subtle (and not so subtle) ways?
- Do you want life to be comfortable, or at least predictable?
- Do you want her to recognize that you have a mind of your own and you know how to use it?
- How well do you really know her?
- Do you even like her?
- Do you hate being told what to do?
- Are you stubborn?
- Are you cheap?

Answer these questions as honestly as you can.

Look for control and power issues. Power struggles are rarely conscious, which is why they can be such a problem. You know what you know, and you think she should know it too. You try to communicate with her, thinking that you're being very clear with words and signals. Too often, you communicate in a vague manner, unable to say what you really mean; and too often, you end up in a yelling match or an emotional standoff with her. She has her own power-struggle issues hiding in her subconscious. Each of you feels the necessity to defend your position. Each of you has different needs to be met. Each of you wants the other to love unconditionally.

You feel angry and misunderstood. "What's the use?" you say. "I'm tired of fighting about the same thing over and over again. I can't take this anymore. Trying to talk to her is like talking to a wall." Frustrated, you or your mate might leave the house, slamming the door on the way out. Or you might clam up, isolate and try to forget it. Even if you calmly agree to disagree, the subject will be revisited. The struggle for power is ruining your relationship, and you feel helpless to do anything about it because you don't even know what the real issue is. The real issue lurks like a ghost in the cobwebs of your childhood brain. The real issue has nothing to do with what you are fighting about.

You've been taught to stand up, suit up, show up, shut up and behave like a man. You've learned that being a man is not only an obligation but also a privilege that comes with having the right sexual apparatus (which you're automatically supposed to know how to use). You're physically stronger and bigger. You have muscles on your muscles.

Your male conditioning starts in the womb with parental expectations. Blue or pink? Trucks or dolls? Footballs or teddy bears? Denim or lace? As a little boy, you develop bravado to protect yourself from being called a girl or a sissy. You learn by ridicule to put on a brave face to conceal physical pain. The primary message you received about being a male was to demonstrate power, brains, might, grit, guts and superiority.

Society expects you to be a warrior. This mandate to be tough kills you—sometimes literally, always metaphorically. You weren't born to be rough, rowdy and rambunctious. You were born to be inventive, imaginative and visionary.

Some women were angry little girls who turned into grade school bullies and terrorized you. You chose not to defend yourself because of a directive not to hit little girls. The men who have shared with me their painful memories about female teachers, babysitters and mothers have unresolved anger about their abuse, and punish all women in very subtle ways. When you uncover the bitterness buried in your soul, you see how it colors all your relationships.

As young boys, you likely set aside or sealed off the emotional part of yourself to fit in or to live up to someone else's idea of you. Certain things were, and still are, expected of you that women typically don't have to worry about. You face the constant pressure to be warriors, protectors, defenders, breadwinners, athletes, company men and leaders. You do your best to take care of your family and your multitude of obligations, but when the lights are out and you want to unwind, your mind is relentlessly telling you that you're not enough. Not wanting to face this, you look for a way to blame someone else. Who's most convenient? Your partner or your boss.

Could it be that some of the antiquated rules you've been following are what're causing the problems in your relationships today? Only you know what those rules are in your life, but here's a typical list:

- Boys don't cry.
- Men should have the last word when a couple is making a decision.
- The one who has the most money has the most power.
- Men are brave and willing to die for a cause.
- Men make the first sexual move.
- It's okay to call a woman a slut or a whore if she dresses like one.
- Men do manly things like hunting and fighting.
- Women's work is the house, the laundry, the kids.
- Women are not to be trusted.
- Men are better drivers.
- Men suffer in silence.

If you've modeled yourself after a father, a coach, a movie star or a fictional hero, you might want to question some of the "rules" you have learned from them. You may be unaware of how much more life has to offer you.

If you grew up without a father, you've had an especially difficult time. It's extremely hard for you to talk about your doubt and confusion because it seems unmanly and weak. You often admit that you don't know who you are or what you're supposed to do. Despite the cultural strides we've all made since the 1960s, the Good Ole Boys Club still exists and your behavior is still influenced by its strong biases, stereotypes, intolerance and narrow points of view. You pay a terrible price for belonging to this club, in terms of both your health and your emotional well-being. You also pay, perhaps, a higher price in ostracism and ridicule if you choose not to be one of the Good Ole Boys.

Perhaps you're hurting and angry because you've been floundering around in your assumptions of what a real man is and does. You've blown off—or have not been able to hear—the complaints of your wife or girlfriend, who may have been telling you for ten, twenty, thirty or more years what would make the relationship good for her. Now that she's given up and is ready to leave, you say, "What can I do to fix this?" You are devastated.

"Too late" she says. "Where were you when I was begging to be heard? Where were your priorities when I was desperately seeking to connect with you? I've already wasted enough time with you."

What you don't know is that she gave up on you years ago. In her fantasy, there is another man who will listen, and she is dying to meet him.

When a woman doesn't get what she wants from a man, sexually and emotionally, she may decide to get it somewhere else, and at the first opportunity. She gives up. You seem to have all the power in the relationship. So she constructs an escape plan, then bides her time until the conditions are right for her to leave.

Now you're both sitting in my office, and she has already emotionally left you. She tolerated you and your obliviousness to her unhappiness for too long. She no longer cares about sex, no longer wants to do things with you and no longer lets your wants dictate her life. You, in turn, have built up a wall of resentment. Oh, you played nice, stayed quiet to keep the peace. You see yourself as the sane one and her as the crazy one. "My conscience is clear," you tell me, while she looks at you with contempt. When you think you're the sensible one, or think you're superior to her and she rejects you, it's a demoralizing blow. Your sense of self is shattered.

Perhaps you never allowed yourself to get close to her or to really see the woman she is. The price you pay for your superiority, for your inattention, is your aloneness. You want some credit for being dutiful and responsible and for the things that you don't do, because "compared to the way my father treated my mother, I am a saint." You get angry when I point out to you that emotionally healthy people don't expect credit for being decent human beings.

CHAPTER 13

Have you ever asked yourself what you want?

Women too have old rules and stereotypes. They are sometimes described are histrionic, mean, cold, designing and dishonest. Others are passive, people-pleasing and wishy-washy. You haven't been able to make sense of your woman's behavior, so you express confusion and disbelief at some of the things taking place in your life.

"What am I supposed to do?' you ask.

The most constructive action you can take is to explore your own beliefs. This means identifying how you are contributing to the problem, and taking inventory of your own behavior. What is the payoff for continuing to live with relational discord?

Women do—and don't—have more freedom than men. Girls aren't teased for wearing boys' clothing or for playing with trucks. Girls can punch little boys and girls can cry, but society places subtle (and not so subtle) pressures and expectations on females too. Parents and teachers influence girls to want feminine things and to behave in manners befitting the weaker sex. Girls are expected to be silly and giggly. Girls are exhorted to do their work quietly and take what is given. Boys are too, but when they act out, they're excused with, "boys will be boys." By her teenage years, your woman learned that men are supposed to make her happy. It is not unusual for girls to start planning their weddings while they are still playing with dolls. The expectation that you can make her happy is the stuff of chick flicks and romance novel. You can certainly influence her happiness, but you can't make her feel any particular way.

You were born into male privilege. Some of you express guilt about this, others resent having it pointed out to them. While females are now encouraged to live up to their potential, women in high places still experience sexism, both overt and covert. Yes, we have come a long way, but our culture has not. Women still earn less than men do for the same job; we take a back seat in the board room, having to maneuver to be listened to. Dr Pamela Coukos, Senior Program Advisor at the Department of Labor's Office of Federal Contract Compliance Programs, reports that " it has been fifty years since Congress mandated equal pay for women, and we still have a pay gap." Forty percent of the pay gap is due to discrimination, sixty percent is due to the difference in jobs. Also, according to the "2011 Annual Report to Congress on the White House Staff," female employees earned 18% less than male employees.

Some women must choose between career and family. Some must choose between husbands and professional opportunities. Others are exhausted by career, household and kids. We would like to think we make autonomous choices, but most of the women I talk with feel torn in a dozen directions. If we don't have children, we're scorned by the people who do. If we are mothers who work outside the home, we feel guilt-ridden for neglecting our children. If we don't want a career, we are always defending our choice to stay home. During quiet times we find ourselves echoing all the critics—parental, cultural, institutional—in our heads. We tolerate sexual innuendos and explicit harassment in the office, and whistles and catcalls on the street. We learned at an early age how to fend off unwanted sexual advances without making waves. We keep quiet about all of it. I know women who work in male-dominated occupations and daily endure belittlement and sexual slurs. Some have even been raped by men in authority. There has been much in the news lately about the enormous number of women in the military who have been raped by men who have sworn to protect this country. Often it is a man of higher rank. But even if the rapist does not have more authority, the person she must report this rape to does, and much of the time her complaints are dismissed with a "boys will be boys" attitude. I had a chance recently to speak to a woman who moved up through the ranks and became an officer of merit. I asked for her thoughts concerning this situation. Her answer: "Yes, it happens all the time. We don't talk about it."

When we walk down the street without a man beside us we are fair game for predators, and in a dark parking lot we must keep all our antennae alert for danger. When there is a rape or a woman is battered, she is often considered the instigator. According to some reports, several hundred women a day are battered, are raped or disappear. Sex traffickers target females as young as three and as old as seventy-five.

You hate all of this as much as we do. You protect us the best way you can, and you loathe the kind of man who abuses women and children. You are respectful, considerate and caring. Still, you don't speak out enough. I saw a sign that said:

Joe is a good hardworking man. He recently broke his leg and was unable to do his work, so the neighbors pitched in and helped him. They also helped him give his wife a broken arm and two black eyes because they knew it was happening and they said nothing.

CHAPTER 14

Men want love too

You grumble about being used and thrown away by the women you love. Some of you claim to be Velcro men, complaining that women who are needy find you and stick to you until they've taken all you have to offer, and then they move on. Your heartsick tales of being cast off like a piece of dirty underwear are very moving. Your grief drives you to isolation or to frantic activity.

How is it that you chose this particular relationship? Are you a hero? A protector? A person who likes to rescue women in distress? Women who are hurting can be very seductive, but starting a relationship with someone because you feel sorry for her is not a good idea. It might feel good in the beginning, but ultimately you are just playing savior. This makes for an unequal balance of power and puts you in a father-like position. When she stops hurting, she will be looking for someone more sexually exciting than a father figure.

Some of you left your wives and children for the fresh excitement of a new love, only to find out the woman you thought you couldn't live without is spoiled and self-serving. Adultery always exacts a price, no matter why you've chosen to do it.

Avoid women who drink a lot, women who gossip about other women and women who flirt outrageously with your friends. Circumvent the woman who wants all of your time and gives up her friends for you. If you are already married to this woman and you are miserable in the relationship, don't use this as an excuse for drinking, taking drugs or spending all your time working. Your feelings, your emptiness, are your responsibility and must be addressed.

If you feel trapped, or in a wearisome cesspool of blunted emotions; if you are no longer in love with her and you are not sure that you every really were; if you fight a lot and sex is non-existent, what are you doing to make things better? If you love her and you don't feel loved in return, then it's time to realize that your way of handling the problem isn't working.

These are, perhaps, some of the issues that you have tried to resolve, all to no avail:
- "I get tired of having to consider her all the time."
- "I try to talk and she won't talk."
- "She never wants to have sex with me."
- "Having sex with her is too much work."
- "She acts like having sex with me is a chore."
- "She has gained a lot of weight and I'm not attracted to her anymore."
- "I can't please her."
- "She corrects me in front of other people."
- "She is too controlling."
- "I'm in love with someone else."
- "She drinks too much."
- "I love her but I'm not in love with her."
- "We don't seem to have anything in common."
- "I'm only staying because I refuse to pay child support."
- "She's crazy."

If you are exhausted by these challenges, it is time to look at your part of the problem. Ignore what she is doing for a while and look at what you are doing. Work on your appearance, your manners and your temperament. Take a good look at what is keeping you in the relationship. What is your payoff for being miserable? There must be one, or you would have made some changes.

She deserves love and so do you. You both deserve respect as well. If neither of you are getting what you deserve, sign up for a couple's retreat or go to relationship counseling. I know, "that costs money," and your ego gets in the way of admitting the size of the problem, but you must do the work. Even if you leave this relationship, you have to take yourself with you.

It is most important that you do not start a relationship with another woman until you can look honestly at what happened with your current or last one.

Remember, love is not a feeling, it's a behavior.

Bill and Linda

Bill and Linda said they were only staying together for the kids. He does his thing and she does hers. Their fourteen-year relationship is fraught with misunderstandings and resentment. They agree on almost nothing, but it wasn't always this way.

In the beginning there was a lot of love. Then Bill lost his job. Linda tried to keep everything going, but watching him get more and more discouraged and bad-tempered created feelings of resentment and self-righteousness in her. She started going out with friends from work to avoid going home at night, and she spent more money than Bill thought she should. He quietly fumed and became more and more depressed. At first, he refused to take a job that paid less than he was making before. Linda was furious with him and started taking sleeping pills because she was lying awake at night worrying about the bills, about the kids and about Bill. Eventually she moved to the guest room.

During a year of therapy, they learned that relationships can never be salvaged by looking for who is to blame. They can be saved, however, if both people work hard to explore their attitudes, beliefs and expectations. Each of them took personal responsibility for the problems in the relationship and agreed to act loving and respectful, even when they did not feel like it.

Bill went back to school to learn a new trade, and Linda stopped staying away from home. She moved back into the bedroom. He joined a men's group, she joined a women's group, and together they agreed to build a new relationship. They planned dates, sex nights and small surprises for each other. Most of all, they learned how to address their problems with a healthy attitude: Bill was not the problem. Linda was not the problem. The problem was the problem. Deliberately changing their attitudes and moving past old expectations resolved most of the difficulty.

The last time I saw them, they were celebrating their twentieth wedding anniversary, dancing cheek to cheek.

Chapter 15

Women want men with class

A man with integrity, dignity and style appeals to all women. A classy man exudes a certain presence, savoir-faire, and graciousness that is immediately palpable when he enters a room.

When you have class, you can be trusted. Your kindness, your quiet authority and your sense of your own value, identity and significance cause you to treat everyone else as if they are special and valuable.

If you're a man with class, you hold the woman you're with as if she's the only woman in the room. You're exceptionally polite to any woman you engage, but you convey non-verbally that you only have eyes for the woman you are with. One very classy man regularly says to me, "Wow! You look sensational tonight, almost as sensational as my wife." I love the compliment and his wife beams. He builds up everyone he talks with, and shows a genuine interest in what is happening in their lives. I never hear a negative word come from his mouth. His gracious manner says, "I am important, and you are just as important."

Classy men don't ogle women on television or on the street, and they don't make sexist remarks—not even in front of other men. When you have class, you are faithful in both word and deed. You can be trusted with secrets and can keep confidences. You don't gossip or engage in false innuendoes or tell tales about past relationships. You're honest in big and small matters. You don't lie, not even by omission or implication. Classy men don't use threats, manipulation or seduction to gain power. When you have class, your power is internally, not externally, derived. Your demeanor and behavior distinguish you from other men. You have principles, and your ethics are apparent in all your dealings with other people.

Some of the things a man with class would never say to a woman are:
- "You look tired."
- "You don't know what you're talking about."
- "You sound awful."
- "You are over-reacting."
- "I don't believe it."
- "What happened to your hair?"
- "You are just like your mother."
- "You women are all the same."
- "It's not my fault."
- "You're the woman. You do it."
- "You can't take a joke."
- "It's not a big deal."
- "Let me show you how it's done."
- "Be reasonable."
- "What do you want now?"
- "Forget it. "

Your poise and self-respect would never allow you to scoff at or ridicule other people. You wouldn't think of repeating gossip, or saying petty things to and about other people. You don't have to put anyone down to lift yourself up or make yourself look better. You would never talk trash about the woman you share your life with. You open doors for women and offer your chair. You ask a woman if she would like help with her coat. You practice good manners, you don't double dip, you don't lick your knife and you know which fork to use for each course of a meal. If you're not sure what constitutes proper etiquette, you politely ask for instruction. You never talk with your mouth full. You tip for service generously and give meaningful, well thought out gifts. Money is a tool you use to make the world a better place.

You know that the old adage, "clothes make the man," is true, not because clothes signal wealth or a hip sense of style, but because they indicate self-respect. You dress tastefully when in public and you know that blue jeans have a place, as does a sport jacket. You wear them when appropriate. You own a good suit or a tuxedo and do not grumble when the occasion calls for such attire.

The man with an edge has an edge, and that edge is class. It's not that a man with class never makes mistakes or faux pas; he does, but he's quick to own them. When you're a classy man, you have humility and you are always ready to learn and grow. Humility isn't self-deprecation, passivity or timidity. Humility is endorsing your whole self, putting any self-consciousness aside and celebrating yourself—and others—as uniquely divine expressions of humanity. Humility is meeting the challenges life offers you head on, and seeing them not as problems, but as projects. Humility means knowing that you can do anything you set your mind to, and do it well if you work hard enough.

You may think this talk of class is outdated, but basic principles of decency and honor don't change just because the culture's attitudes shift. Nor do they change because some women give you the hairy eyeball when you open the door for them. A woman's post-feminist defiance and un-classy behavior doesn't excuse you from behaving with the integrity that aligns with your values.

You can dress well, display good manners, say all the right things, pretend to be gracious and still not have class because your priorities and your values will tell the truth about you. False pride, negative smugness and egotism are the antithesis of class. A man with class would never allow friends, outsiders, or neighbors to feel sorry for his mate because she is married to him.

Winning a woman's trust, respect and devotion is easier than you think. Be exactly who you are. Always tell the truth. Be open and available to listen to her and share your real feelings. Be curious and adventurous and a bit of a risk taker. Seek new challenges and experiences. Develop your sense of humor. Women love men who know how to dance, so learn. And it also won't hurt to learn how to be an accomplished, masterful lover.[4]

---

[4] "Masterful: Powerful, skillful, master of technique." From *The American Heritage Dictionary of the English Language*, edited by William Morris, American Heritage Publishing Company Inc., 1969.

CHAPTER 16

Foreplay: the mark of a masterful lover

Foreplay. The word has been recorded since the 1920s, but historical references to it and artistic depictions of it are centuries old. Women and men need foreplay to have great sex. And while each of us may need it to varying degrees in any given moment, day, year or decade, foreplay should be an integral part of the daily behavior of a fully functioning relationship. Yes, daily.

If you want to have more and better sex with your woman then you have to talk about it with her. Talk can be a frightening four-letter word, and you might have to practice talking about sex out loud, in front of a mirror, before you can bring yourself to discuss it with her.

Choose a time when you are sitting side by side in a car or on the couch, which will feel less confrontational for both of you than when you are facing off across a table or standing. And don't expect this conversation to lead immediately to sex. You're just talking. To create safety, establish these ground rules: If either of you hears something that hurts, you won't get defensive; and if feelings do escalate, you'll table the conversation until you're both calm and recommitted to mutual understanding. Share your thoughts and feelings about sex, your needs and hang-ups, your satisfactions and dissatisfactions, and invite her to share her own. Make no assumptions. Listen from an open heart and mind as you likely did when you first met her.

Sexuality has historically been an anxious and troubled territory for women, so she may not want to discuss, or be able to tell you, or even know for herself what she wants and needs. Encourage her gently to communicate whatever and however she can. Sex must be a safe topic at all times. There are a number of books and DVDs for couples, but avoid hard-core porn as it denigrates the beauty of sex.

When communicating about sex, bold truth-telling is critical, because if either of you has been withholding resentments or fears, it will be difficult to find the freedom and abandon needed for healthy, robust foreplay.

Here are some pertinent questions for both of you to ask yourselves:

- What am I self-conscious, embarrassed or ashamed about in my sexual self?
- Do I worry about my body (e.g., weight, aging or imperfections)?
- Do I worry about my performance (e.g., premature ejaculation, inexperience or inhibitions)?
- Am I lusty or do I lack libido?
- Do I know how to be romantically assertive and not wishy-washy about my desire?
- What physical, hormonal, psychological or emotional issues contribute to my issues with sex or my lack of performance?
- How am I contributing to the sexual dissatisfaction in my relationship?
- Am I resigned, passive, unresponsive or controlling?
- Do I reject my partner's sexual advances or withhold sex?
- Am I afraid to expand my sexual knowledge and techniques?
- Do I disengage by using alcohol, drugs or overwork?
- Do I talk insensitively about previous lovers and sexual experiences?
- Have I bragged about my sexual prowess with a previous lover?
- Have I ignored messages from my partner that something is missing in our sexual relationship?
- What messages about sex have I inherited from my family and my culture?
- Have I been a victim of sexual abuse?
- What, ideally, do I need to be sexually satisfied?

- Have I told her?

You and your woman can't please each other if you don't tell or show each other what you want, in and out of the bedroom. Foreplay is not only sexy talk, teasing affectionately, and sensual touch, but respect, compliments, praise, encouragement and any intimate behaviors that say, "I know you, and I love what I know." Foreplay is noticing when something needs to be done, and doing it. Foreplay is never letting her doubt your devotion and attraction to her.

Your sex life can be amazing and exhilarating just by adding some skills:

- Cradle her in a wordless embrace at least once a day.
- Offer to take showers or baths together.
- Shave your stubble if it irritates you woman's skin.
- Brush your teeth and use mouthwash if your breath needs additional freshening.
- Soften rough, calloused hands with cream or lotion and trim your fingernails.
- Offer a back rub or a foot rub.
- Prop yourself up on a couple of pillows against the bed's headboard, invite her to lie against your naked body and slowly and delicately caress her skin.
- Kiss her eyelids and breathe into her hair.
- Kiss the hollows of her neck and linger there.
- Synchronize your breathing with hers.
- Invite her to lie on top of you while you massage her back.
- Touch and kiss the other parts of her body before moving to her breasts and genitals.
- Gently touch and suck her nipples, and lick the area between her breasts.
- Lightly rest your palm on her genitals.
- Be aware of your weight; don't lie on her like a heavy blanket.
- Ask for what you want (e.g., a different position, oral sex or cuddling). Tell her how to touch you and where.

Foreplay without romance is empty technique, and romance means different things to different women. Not all women want roses or candlelight dinners, but every single one wants to feel loved and understood. Romance is about connection, smells, touching and wordless recognition. Romance is born with lots of love, acceptance and encouragement to dream, to indulge in fantasy, to accept the desires in your heart and to delight in who you are. The emotionally available man is proud of his ability to love with passion, warmth and desire. If you are this man, you aim to live life to the fullest. You don't have hidden agendas or concealed issues. You love with confidence and conviction. You take the time to learn what your woman wants.

CHAPTER 17

What women say they want from their men

The advice in this chapter is based on hundreds of counseling hours. It will be helpful to you whether you are in a new relationship or have been married for fifty years. Don't try to do it all at once, though. Pick one behavior and do it often and until it becomes second nature. Then pick another one, and continue until you have learned them all. You will be amazed at how your relationship blossoms.

Here are the things that women want:
- To be heard and understood.
  Say, "I hear you, I see you. Please help me understand how this is important to you. This conversation won't be over until I get what you're saying."
- Tell her you appreciate the sacrifices she makes for you.
  Say, "I know that you went out of your way to make my life a little easier today. Thank you for doing_____."
- Ask her what she wants in a loving way.
  Ask, "What is it you want, and how can I help you get it?"
- Say clearly what you want from her.
  Say, "I would really appreciate it if you

would_____, because I need_____."

- Don't assume that you know what she wants, especially if the assumption is based on your experience with other women. Ask, "What makes you feel loved? Flowers? Cards? Gifts? Time?"
- Pick up after yourself.
- Say, "Sorry about the _____ laying there. I'll take care of it right now."
- Always present a united front in public. If she speaks or acts inappropriately, discuss it in private.
- Tell her, "I've got your back. No matter what, you can count on me."
- Don't duck and run when she is angry with you. Offer to listen.
- Ask, "Are you mad about something? Is this a good time to talk about it?"
- Compliment her in public in front of her friends.
- Say, "Doesn't she look beautiful?" or "She is the smartest person I know."
- Reassure her that she is the only woman for you.
- Tell her, "You are the only woman for me. No one else can hold a candle to you in my eyes."
- When she is not present, say only positive things about her.
- Say, "I am a better man because of her. I am really proud of her."
- Don't talk about your ex-wife or former lovers, unless it is to help your current relationship.
- Say: "My ex-wife called me out on my sarcastic tone, so please let me know if I speak disrespectfully to you."

Your woman wants you to stand up for your values and beliefs, to walk your talk. She wants you to honor your commitments over your impulses, and to hold yourself accountable when you screw up. She wants you to face problems with courage, and she wants you to recognize that you're part of some mysterious, divine scheme for this world. She wants you know that you are valuable, worthwhile and indispensable to her and the children. She wants you to understand that devoting yourself to the world's needs, your job's needs or even her needs, while suppressing your own, will ultimately destroy you. She wants you to take care of yourself.

She wants you to be a mature adult male who refuses to indulge in childish grudges or get-even tactics. She wants to be able to look up to you and respect and admire your principles.

She wants you to know that she recognizes the monumental responsibility and pressures of being a man in this world. She wants you to respect money and use it wisely, not worship it. She wants you to care about all of life, and do what you can to help abused children and homeless people. She wants you to cultivate your emotional, psychological and spiritual health. She wants you to have an open mind and to try new challenges. She wants you to love your life. She wants you to live in your truth and encourage others to live in theirs. She wants you to thrive, not just survive. She wants you to put your life in perspective, be grateful for what you have and focus on doing the next right thing.

SECTION THREE

Real Women, Real Stories

The following stories are true. Please allow some poetic license as each one is, as much as possible, just as it was written or dictated by a woman who is willingly sharing her life and her experiences with you. I hope their stories will inspire and embolden you. Glean what you can use from them to empower yourself to be all that you can be.

Mandy

My wants and needs are complex because my world has become complex. It is my perception that more and more is continually being demanded of me. I cannot keep up. Where do I belong? I do not know. At the end of my life, I would like to know concretely that I have changed some small element of my world for the better. Contributing to society is important to me. I would like to know that I have made a difference in a good and meaningful way. Maybe I could make a huge difference by doing social work.

More importantly, I would like to make a difference in the life of at least one individual. To share with others some measure of the knowledge I have gained, so that someone else can benefit from it. I would also like to know that the children I have brought into the world and raised are happy people who help to bring happiness to those important to them. What I have given to my children is the star that I want to shine the brightest. I want my treatment of my children to be my claim to having produced some good in this world.

From my work, I want to know that I am valued for the contribution that I make. To me, family is the career and work is something that allows my family to be in a better place. I've been torn with guilt because, in actuality, I believe that my family would have been in a better place had I not worked.

But I did what I did with them in mind, so it is done. Now I work to allow me to do some things I have never done. I am thinking about using work as a way to move around the country so I can experience new places. I have to feel productive in a job or I probably could not stay with it.

What I want from a man is a hard to define, because to draw attention to myself in that way makes me very uncomfortable. I have difficulty trusting. Is anything more than first sexual instinct asking too much? From a man—father, husband, brother or friend—I would like to feel that I am the recipient of his respect. I want to be appreciated for the person that I am, for my knowledge, for my ability and for my feeling. Without respect, there is no love. The respect must be given for who I am, not for the things I do or what I can produce.

I think respect is vital to the relationship of a husband and wife. What comes from that respect are love and the union of selves to produce an ultimate bond. I want to be free to be who I am, to be an individual in union with my husband to produce an entity that is stronger and more complete than either of us apart. In our union, I want each of us to contribute to making the other more—not better, just more.

What I want in a physical way from a man is twofold. I want shiver, tingle and throb and I want to make him feel good, feel loving, feel like screaming, feel tender and to feel in love. I want to feel loved; I want to be the point of all his concern and his care. I want to feel that I am a partner with him. I do not want to be made to feel like an object that is only there to wait on him or to give him enjoyment.

It is very important to me to feel that we are both working toward a common goal. I want us to be of like mind so we can combine efforts to do something meaningful. I derive my enjoyment from joint accomplishment. I like working together, fixing that fence, painting the house or entertaining friends.

My family of origin and the family I conceived have been a huge disappointment for me. My parents set a standard for our family, and it hurts me that there are those who do not keep in contact with one another. There is little tolerance for siblings who are of different minds from the majority. The closeness that existed when we were young is no longer there. The effort of trying to be accepted or to be heard is frustrating, and wears away at the very core of my self-worth. I want us to be close as a family as we edge toward the end of our lives. I want my family's support in the issues in my life and I want to be able to give support. I just want to belong.

I would like my own children to communicate with me and with one another. I would like them to understand that each person is in a different circumstance and that each has to live by their own set standards and not be judged by the others. I want to see my children support one another in their lives. I want to be allowed to be in their lives. As it is, even with my large family of origin and with all my children and grandchildren, I feel so very alone. I want to love and be loved and respected as a mom, grandmother, aunt and sister. I don't know how to make that happen.

Above all else, I want to be happy. I know it is up to me to choose what will make me happy. I think I know what will make me happy; I just need to figure out how to get it. I hope it won't take as long to get it as it has taken me to figure it out.

Brenda

I think that what I want might sound silly to other people because on the surface it looks as if I have everything any woman could want. I live in a beautiful house. My children are well behaved. We go to church every Sunday and take vacations together every year. My husband is a hard worker, though he's also pretty self-centered and opinionated. Ten years ago, when we met, he was seductive, reckless, exciting and full of praise, respect, compliments and attention. Now he treats me like an appendage.

I'm wickedly, carnally, physically attracted to his broad shoulders, his long legs and his mass of curly hair. Once I was crazy in love with him; sometimes still, when I am sitting next to him the smell of his body fills me with so much desire I can hardly breathe. I love the pungent musky smell of him. It sounds funny, but when he sits down beside me or lies beside me in bed, I am sucked in. His scent takes my breath away and leaves me feeling helpless.

In the beginning, we'd have sex four and five times a day, and I'd eventually get to an orgasm. Most often now, I have sex with him and then turn to the wall feeling that it's all pointless. I have tried to make suggestions to him about things he could do to make sex better, but he can't seem to hear me. As long as he is satisfied, that is all that really matters to him. He doesn't seem to realize, or maybe he doesn't care, that our sex life could be great if I felt like he treasured me; I want to feel cherished. I want to be adored. Hell, I want to have a real orgasm.

He decides what we do socially. He makes unilateral decisions without consulting me; in addition, he seems to be convinced that he knows what is best for everyone. He shows a lot of disdain for people who don't agree with him. He sometimes says that I am boring him or he makes jokes about me. He accuses me of being too sensitive when he says something that cuts me deeply, usually about something I can't help, like my big nose, my small breasts or my family. He is the one with the big nose!

I do many things for him, hoping to attract his attention. He acts as if he's entitled to whatever I give him. I want him to get a clue and do the same things for me. He often has an excuse for not doing anything much for me. He blames circumstances, or says he doesn't have any money or that he ran out of time. I live with him knowing that he doesn't really see me or care about my needs and my heartaches, with a peculiar kind of suffering that has no name.

Kelly

My father was a humble dairy farmer whom I worshiped. My mother was a talented singer who came from a long line of musicians. There weren't many opportunities available in our small, homey community for a little girl, but my mother, wise and wonderful woman that she was, made sure that I had tap dancing and piano lessons. Getting me to the lessons every week on time and in the proper get-up was her way of indulging both of us in her love for music. She could belt out some amazingly beautiful sounds and was always in demand for weddings, funerals and musical entertainment in our town of seven hundred.

I loved to dance, so it broke my heart when my tap dancing teacher moved away, leaving me a has-been at the age of seven. Full of passion for music and dance, I used to invite my girlfriends over to join me in our farmhouse basement to spend hours dancing. Funny, they didn't always share my mania, so sometimes it was just me doing the best I could to entertain myself, lost in la la land with Elvis.

I discovered the drums in sixth grade, thanks to a friend who twisted my arm to join band with her. My life changed then, and aspirations of being a rock star kicked in. I told my dad this and he bought me a full, shiny drum set. I didn't quite know what to do with them; I had only played the snare drum in school. Every time I fooled around with the drum set, I ended up feeling inadequate and lost. I didn't know what to do. Who could teach me what to do? I eventually sold them; I had no clue that in the years to come, I would beat myself up and kick myself around many blocks for doing this. My regret was palpable and ate at me in unsuspecting moments.

I played the piano through all twelve years of school, doing the music for all types of band and chorus events. And I battled my weight. Being a big girl is very hard in high school. When it was time to graduate, I had no idea where to go or what I wanted to be. I choose the lesser of several evils and went to business school. I was quite heavy by then. Tall, big and heavy. Inside me was a steamy, skinny woman with a rekindled passion for dancing. I ached to set free that thin, beautiful creature who kept crying for release. It was a hunger I shared with no one.

Young and seeking life, I found myself in many bars. One night my world was altered, revolutionized, because I was mesmerized by the sight of an all-girl band. Oh my god, I could've been in an all-girl band if I had just kept my drum set! My heart throbbed and burned with remorse, sorrow, regret and self-reproach. I set a new goal to go back to playing the drums, to be in an all-girl band and, of course, to be a rock star. In my head I was svelte, desirable and famous, but in my mirror I was a yo-yo in terms of weight. Sometimes two hundred pounds, sometimes less.

On my way to fame, I became a bartender. Alcohol and drugs masked the ache in my heart. In the dark, stinky bar reeking of smoke and booze, my self-esteem was zilch. At least I got to meet men and listen to a lot of music. I couldn't stand myself. I dropped off the path of self-respect and found the road to destruction and heartache. My body was lumpy and disgusting to me. My hair was curly, fuzzy, a big jumbled uncooperative mess, and my fat loomed in buffeting bumps despite my best efforts to avoid seeing it. I was loud and obnoxious. I accepted the only love available—guys who came on to me in the bar while they were drunk and wanted a piece of me. One day I reached the end of my endurance; I felt unacceptable and was failing at the game of life.

I turned to God. He was the only one I knew I could trust. Down on my knees, I threw myself on His mercy. "God," I prayed, "please, please help me get my life together. I hate myself. Please send me some help. Please send me a good honest, drug-free man and a different way of life. I can't live this way anymore."

I swear by all that is Holy, He heard me. He heard me and He answered me. Very soon I accepted a date with a man who'd actually asked me out hundreds of times. I had always said no because he was married, but this time I relented and agreed to go. Dressed and ready I waited, only to be stood up. Oh yeah, that was the best day of my life.

I went by myself to see a band at a local bar. Feeling lonely and rejected, I noticed a man watching me. God does know what He is doing, because my life changed the moment I danced with the man who is now my husband. He is everything I asked God for and then some. We have been together now for thirty years, and there have been a lot of ups and downs and twists and turns. He believes in me. He helps guide me. He supports my dreams.

He loved me fat and now he loves me slim. He loves me senseless and he loves me rational. He has given up so much so I could dance. Sometimes I can see that it almost sucks the life out of him.

A week after meeting my husband-to-be, I saw an ad for belly dancing classes at the YMCA. I was intrigued. I had to investigate. Could this be something to appease the hunger for movement and music inside of me? Could this satisfy my wanton appetite for rhythm and sexual expression? Would it allow me to move? I didn't have a clue what it was, but I went right down to sign up. I was desperate for motion and musical movement.

Belly dancing has totally changed my life. It gives me discipline. It demands the structure I want and shows me that many different types of women can come together. Women who belly dance are all ages and come from all different walks of life. We would probably never meet each other under any other circumstances. Belly dancers bond. We have each other's backs, we support each other, we share paraphernalia if needed—and we dance.

Blissful is the way to describe my life. I'm a professional belly dancer and I dance for literally thousands of people. I have my own small business teaching others how to belly dance. It's hard to make a living doing this anywhere, and in the middle of cowboy country it is even harder. My husband often has to carry the load financially and sometimes he isn't happy about it. He sacrifices for me monetarily and suffers a lot of disappointment because I put my dancing first.

My husband, used to be a street fighter who settled everything with his fists. He's capable of saying some very hurtful things but, at the end of the day, he works tirelessly to help me set up and tear down shows, move equipment, carry costumes, and make sure everything is in order. I could never begin to repay him for all the love, work and hardship he has gone through for me. Yet it wasn't enough. I whined to my husband—and whoever else would listen—about not being able to play the drums. Even though I'd long ago given up the idea of being a rock star, I felt incomplete. Whenever I saw a drummer, especially if it was a woman, I was consumed with envy. I'd say, "I wish that was me. I could be doing that." I didn't do anything about it, I just bellyached. I had no drums. I couldn't afford them. A good drum set costs a zillion dollars; at least it seemed like a zillion to me. The worst thing, though, is that I had no confidence.

I dreamed about it, I thought about it, I prayed about it and finally I screwed up my courage. With a hammering heart and shortness of breath, I asked my husband if he would loan me the money to buy a good set of drums. I almost collapsed on the floor with gratitude when he said, "I've been wanting to buy you something. Why don't I just get them for you?" Is it any wonder I am head over heels crazy about this man? He gets me. He reinforces me, he validates me. Every woman should have a man like the one God sent me.

At the age of 59, with arthritis in both hands, I fell in love with a splendiferous set of shiny new drums. They sparkle like silver eye shadow and twinkle in the light like a thousand stunning stars gleaming with luminescent flitters. My heart could barely contain my joy. I sought drumming teachers. I know I was overwhelming to them. How could they understand a forty-year longing finally finding fulfillment? At first, I was so flighty I would forget my drumsticks and leave my keys in the car. Who cares? I was seeing my dream come alive.

Even though I'm never going to be the drummer for Deep Purple, my teacher has shown me a completely new world and I am having the time of my life. He takes me on jobs where an extra percussionist is needed—and this is heady stuff for this woman.

Dancing continues to be my passion. I teach belly dancing to a large number of spirited, loyal, whimsical women of every age and every size. I create finger cymbal and tambourine routines and drum while they dance. I do the choreography for all our public appearances. It is exquisitely satisfying.

Sometimes in life, a person has to take control and do things that are not pretty. One of my sad experiences involved another woman who was also a belly dance teacher. She expended an enormous amount of energy badmouthing me and attempting to ruin my business by stealing clients and opportunities for shows. I put up with it for a long time, ignoring her and turning the other cheek. However, after several years of this I put a stop to it. Screwing up all my courage, I threatened her with a lawsuit and told her my brother-in-law was president of a well-known biker gang. One of these things got her attention. No more rumors reached my ears.

I'm a woman who goes after what she wants, but I don't get it at other people's expense. I don't believe in hurting other people. I believe God is my helper and my strength. I believe in giving others a hand up and the benefit of the doubt. Sometimes in belly dancing the focus gets skewed when women that are insecure and jealous of other women place more importance on looks and body shape than they do on being a good human being and treating others with respect. It is ironic how I went from someone that was overweight, undisciplined and disrespectful of me—and everyone else—to a woman who teaches the exact opposite.

I will go to my grave battling my weight. So will many other women. I tell other women to accept themselves as they are and to celebrate being alive. Some women are repressed and demoralized by rigid messages of sin, and are told to hide their bodies and behave in ways that do not attract attention to them. I encourage them to love themselves and to believe in themselves and, in so doing, I realize there is nothing wrong with the way I look, even though it is a constant battle in my head. I am so thankful for my life. I do not know how much more content I could possibly be.

My husband, bless his heart, has learned that if I ask, "do I look fat in this outfit?" to say very carefully, "I've seen you in other outfits that I like better." Who could ask for a finer man? My father once told me that you never measure a man's success by his pocketbook. I have never forgotten those words of wisdom. I am more blessed and more successful than I ever could have imagined. I could tell you hundreds of belly dancing stories, but that would be a book in itself. The one I will share with you is the feeling I get when I take someone from the first day of class to a full-blown performing artist. I don't have children, but I suspect it is the same feeling parents gets when they see their child accomplish something such as a graduation. The joy I feel when I see a woman I am working with grow into a well-rounded, controlled, passionate belly dancer is beyond explanation. So many women have signed up for classes and then quit when they realize belly dancing is actually hard work—and if they don't have rhythm it is especially hard. Some of them try it few times, then discover that it takes perseverance and a willingness to look foolish at first. Unfortunately, they do not give their bodies a chance to find out what it is like to be truly sensual, even sultry. But when they do, they grow into women who truly love their bodies and believe in themselves. Belly dancing is an art form like no other.

The one thing I can offer to other women is this: if you want something, go after it. Let nothing get in your way. And do it with God's blessing and support.

Judy

I want my husband to treat me as well as he treats our dog. Admittedly, our little spaniel is special and I love her too, but when my husband comes home from work in the evening, he blows kisses to our daughter, grunts a weary "hi" at me and then talks to the dog. "Ahhh," he coos. "How's you today? Did you miss me?" Sometimes he brings her a treat, whipping it out of a brown paper bag with a flourish, while she barks and jumps up and down. He makes a big deal out of giving it to her. Then he heads for the bathroom. I ache, I hurt and I mourn while pretending this doesn't matter. After all, what kind of a woman is jealous of a dog? Where is my brown paper bag with a surprise? He hasn't brought me flowers for years. When he comes out of the bathroom, he sits down in the recliner with our dog in his lap and cuddles her. Eyes straight ahead on the evening news, just him and the dog, lost in his own little world. Sometimes our daughter will go and climb in the recliner with them, but if she disturbs the dog she is reprimanded. I watch this night after night. I wonder what I would have to do to get this kind of attention. I feel so resentful of that dog I have even plotted to run over her. I think devious thoughts of how to get rid of her, but then sanity prevails and I know it is not the dog but my husband. Then I think briefly about the satisfaction I would feel if I ran over him instead of the dog. I want my husband to hurt as badly as I do.

I wonder how to connect with him. It seems like all my approaches to him are met with a "what do you want now?" attitude. No matter how much I try to explain to him that I am aching with loneliness from the lack of affection and the coldness between us, I cannot seem to get him to understand. So then I ask myself, am I ugly? Am I too fat? Am I dumb? Does he not find me attractive at all? What is wrong with me? I often go to bed alone—or he does. Occasionally he wants sex, but why would I want to have sex with a man who ignores me? Sometimes we do it on a Friday night. When we are finished, I feel even emptier than I did before we started. I don't know how he feels because he doesn't tell me. I have a suspicion that he might be homosexual. Once, in a burst of anger about his lack of desire for me, I said, "What the hell is going on? Are you gay?" I never got an answer to this, only a complete and total shutout, the silent treatment, for the rest of the week.

When I try to tell him how I feel, he turns a deaf ear and calls me a nag. My needs are a bother to him. He says he is too tired to deal with me. The dog asks for nothing, and no matter how he treats her, she wags her tail and runs to him. How do I compete with that? I have actually thought about meeting him at the door on all fours, barking up a storm and licking his face. I wonder what would happen? Probably he would say, "I knew it! You're nuts!"

When I tell him I am unhappy with him he says, "You're crazy. You don't know how good you have it. I work hard, I don't screw around and I bring you all the money."

"Yes," I scream, "but you do not talk to me. You don't tell me what is going on. What is wrong with you?"

A superior look and a smile is all I get in response, and then, as if I have said nothing, he asks, "What are you fixing for dinner?"

Therefore, here is what I want. I want a warm-hearted acceptance and a sense of humor in the face of my screw-ups. I want to feel secure in his love and acceptance, and confident of his good will toward me. I want to be protected by his strength and to know that I am loved. I want to feel appreciated. I want to be understood. I want at least as much tenderness and attention as I see him giving the dog.

Sexually, I want to feel alive and desirable. I want to have sex with someone who tells me that he loves my body, someone who notices when I wear lacy nightgowns and pretty panties and sexy bras. I want him to buy me some racy underwear and perfume. My husband does not know the meaning of the word "foreplay." Sex to him is a two-minute warm-up: kiss her, touch her breasts and go for the gold. Early in our relationship, I tried to talk to him about sex, but neither of us could get past our hang-ups to have a real discussion. I wanted oral sex. He felt disgusted by that, even though he likes that I am willing to do it for him. I suggest books and videos and he seems mildly interested at the thought, but does not follow up. I am embarrassed about our sex life and his lack of desire. I know there is so much more that we could be enjoying. I often daydream about having an affair. If the right man comes along, I might do it. In fact, I daydream about the man, what he would look like, the romantic way he would treat me, the amorous, slow undulating sex we share, while he tells me I am beautiful and he can't live without me. Sometimes my husband sees me staring into space and he calls my name a couple of times before I respond. "There you go thinking again," he says. If he only knew!

Molly

What do I want? I have lived with this question since you asked it of me, much longer than I would have thought necessary. I find it is not an easy question to answer. I thought of all sorts of things, and when I sat down to write, the question was just so daunting. What do I want? It is unsettling to look at my wants, and I found myself feeling less than satisfied with my answers. I almost chucked the whole thing. After all, who wants to do that much soul searching or work that hard? I sometimes fall into the trap of, "I want what I want when I want it, and I want it now."

Over the years, I have come to realize that desires are like tyrants—they demand more and more of my energy and leave me feeling empty. It isn't material things that are of great importance; rationally, I know that. To paraphrase Paul from the Bible who wrote in Romans, "I do the things I don't want to do, and the things I want to do I don't do." I relate to Paul in this matter. It is so hard to fall short of who I want to be. I know I cannot be who I want to be on my own, but with God I can.

The things I want from friends include loyalty, love, honesty, respect, sincerity and humor. From my husband I want the same and even more. I want my husband to walk beside me and share in the faith that God has given us. I want him to help me live a life of peacefulness. I delight in my husband's sense of humor; I relish his laughter and love it when he is happy.

From my sisters I want loyalty, encouragement and honesty. If my hairstyle needs changing or my pants are too tight, I want them to tell me. I want to continue to laugh with them until our sides hurt and we almost wet our pants. I want to feel the mirth that is the invisible connection of blood and shared memories.

What I really want came to me in church as I was listening to the songs. Deep in my heart, I want to be still, no matter what is going on in the world, in my city, with my family or with my husband. I want to be still and feel God's power at work in my life. I want to be still and know that everything is okay because God is in charge. I want to love God with all my heart, all my soul and with my entire mind as scripture commands me to do. I want Jesus. I want the deep sensation that He is holding me and that everything is okay.

I want to be still and spend time listening to God. I do not do it as often as I might. I forget and let other things get in my way. I get too busy taking care of other people and using up my energy in various ways. Sometimes I try too hard to make other people happy.

My life has been one of trial and tragedy, with moments of exquisite joy. I wouldn't be honest if I denied wanting to do over parts of my life. I mean, who doesn't? There is a lot of "if only" in my life and a do over was one of the first things I thought of when you asked me what I want. I have a deep regret that surfaces from time to time, for example, when I visit a doctor's office. When I go to the doctor, one of the questions that is always asked of me is how many pregnancies and births I have had. When this question comes, my gut and my heart do flip-flops. I am ashamed. I am scared of what they will think of me when I say I have had two abortions. I don't want to have to tell them. I don't want it to be true. Even though I had good reason, there is no chance to explain; there is only the cold hard fact.

For a long time I tried to pretend that the abortions never happened. I kept the information close to my heart, and thought if I didn't acknowledge it, perhaps it would go away and not be true. To help it go away, I drank. A lot, and then some more.

Sitting in a twelve-step recovery meeting last week—once again living the question of what I want--I told this group of women that the time I spend with them is sacred time and I want more of it. I want to continue to see how God is at work in my life and in the lives of the other women in the group. I have so much compassion for these women who, like me, have made choices that caused a lifetime of pain. I can help them because of my experiences, and I want very much to do it.

I can have sex now without having alcohol first. I like sex. I believe that lovemaking is a gift from God. When my husband and I have sex, we pray first. When we first started doing this, my husband was very skeptical about it. Actually, I think he thought I was nuts. I lead the prayers, ask God to renew our lovemaking and then I praise Him and thank Him for this beautiful gift. For us it has increased our intimacy and helped us respect the power of prayer.

Recently, I have been humbled by the fact that my sister allowed me to have the sex talk with my preteen nieces. I explained to them how God made our bodies so that we can be a gift to each other. I detailed how God created the chemistry, the excitement and the bodily responses. I wanted them to know that, for me, God is a part of every good thing in life.

God has given me so much—so much healing and so much of everything else, emotionally, physically and materially. When I contemplate my life today, I wonder who I would be without all my previous experience, both good and bad. I want to further my connection with the God of my understanding and worship the triune Father, Son, and Holy Spirit. I want to know God's will and have the power to carry it out.

This question of what I want has brought me to my knees. It has jumped all over inside of me. The gamut of emotions that surge and swirl has made me realize that whatever it is that I want, I am the one who needs to take the steps to accomplish it. Right now, I want to get better organized and I have made some plans to do that. Thank you for the opportunity to live this question.

Cheryl

For twenty-three years, I was cowed by my first husband. We had a marriage based on his needs. I didn't know what love was then, so I don't think I ever loved him. Life settled into a monotonous routine. I thought children would make our marriage better, so we had two of them. Later, I realized what I now had was two more innocent people to protect from a verbally and emotionally abusive man. He never hit me, but I always felt bruised and beat up. There was no way to please him.

My husband was very controlling, and he thought that if I was not at work, I should be home and happy to be there. The verbal punishment was so harsh that I soon learned it was easier just to stay home and give up family and friends. I shaped my life around his needs and handed over my life to keep the peace.

Sex with my husband was as exciting as a root canal. He was selfish and thought foreplay was too much trouble, so I was always left feeling incomplete and used. In the beginning, when I still thought he cared, I would try to tell him how it felt to be so mentally and spiritually abused. Later, I was just numb and cold toward the idea of sex with him, and would avoid going to bed until after he was asleep as often as I could. When that didn't work, I suffered through it, watching the clock until he got his rocks off and I could be left alone.

The thought of any other life never crossed my mind. It is difficult to feel like a worthwhile human being when the one who is supposed to love and protect you constantly tells you how worthless and stupid you are. He told me I was lucky to have him because no one else would put up with me.

One day I received a message concerning my mother. She had died. Mother had long been the center of my life and of my siblings' lives. She was only sixty-four years old when she died. Why? In her house during the days that followed her death, I kept thinking, "Is this all there is to life? What is it all for? Could she have lived longer if my father had treated her better?"

Up to this point, I had tried to be a buffer between my husband and my boys, and to shield them from knowing how unhappy I was. Suddenly I knew that I was fighting for my life and I could no longer stay in an abusive marriage if I wanted to live longer than my mother had. I knew I had to leave, no matter the cost—and it was considerable. My husband was first disbelieving, and then threatening, then pleading, then furious and he played the victim with my boys. Unexpectedly, I became the bad guy, and was blamed for their father's sadness and dejection. I felt bad for them. They could not know how bad it was for me because I'd protected them and had not let them know. But now I could not waste any more of my life in a relationship that was sucking the life out of me.

My life changed dramatically. I was happier single than I'd been for a very long time. The ease of being able to come and go at will, coupled with the freedom from the constant verbal assaults, gave me rest and peace of mind. I hurt for my boys and wanted them to understand, but that was out of my hands.

I also missed my mother terribly. My grief was staggering. My sister told me that Mom used to tell her she was worried that I was being mistreated in my marriage. I wish she could have told me that herself; I might have realized the importance of getting out sooner.

Four years after my divorce I met and married my second husband and I consider him God's gift to me. He is a real man. He shows me what a marriage is supposed to be. We are true partners in everything—soul mates, if you will. He genuinely considers my feelings and my needs. He is a thoughtful, considerate, generous, exciting lover. It is a talented man who knows how to make love to a woman. The best ones really like women's bodies and are willing to learn how to please. My husband is a foreplay expert. I never turn him down.

My second husband's parents were great role models for him. I encourage anyone thinking about getting married to look at the parents of the person you want to marry. Will they make good grandparents? Are they kind and compassionate? Do they treat each other well?

I wish my mother could see me now. I wonder if she knows how happy I am. I wonder if she knows that her death made me realize that life is precious and I am the one who has to make it worth living. I want to believe she sees me every day and is cheering for me.

My prayer is that every woman can know how valuable and worthwhile she is, and that if she chooses to get married she can find a great mate like the one I have. You cannot marry a person hoping he will change, nor can you teach one how to love you if he is not willing to learn. You can't stop an angry, hurtful person from taking the venom out on you. You can only refuse to be a victim.

I pray that my sons have not been warped by the years of listening to the poison spewed from their father's mouth. I pray they will have lives of fulfillment and accomplishment. I am grateful that they eventually came around and accepted my second husband. I know they see his good manners and generosity, and now have a better idea of how a real man behaves. I want them to know God. I want them to have a quality life. I want them to know that real men have no need to abuse women—verbally or physically.

Barbara

I met Mike just before Christmas when my friend dragged me to his company party. The party, full of holiday music and excitement, promised me only a break from the mad hurried shoppers and endless people I was forced to deal with on a daily basis. The decorations were elaborate and extravagant. The food and drink were sumptuous, the music soft and romantic and I felt beautiful in my figure-caressing green velvet gown.

Mike appeared from out of nowhere. I did not see him until the evening was nearing an end. Something drew my gaze in his direction. Not exactly handsome but not homely either, he flashed me an appealing grin. He boasted a mop of dark hair with enough silver to be distinguished; he had broad shoulders and a trim waistline. I didn't know who he was, but I could feel him watching me. Moving toward me to ask me to dance, he walked with an air of superb confidence. When we danced, he moved with fluid grace, like Patrick Swayze. He knew of his ability to please a woman in a way that few men can, and it showed in his walk. Women of all ages came on to him as if they knew the secret of his rare ability.

On our first date, he presented me with champagne and flowers. He treated me like a unique treasure. He insisted on opening the car door, pulling out my chair and standing until I was seated. Later, he teased my senses, holding my face in his hands, kissing me lightly, gently, blowing on the back of my neck, kissing my fingers and groaning when we kissed good night.

On the second date, we danced cheek to cheek. He pulled me to him and in effortless, graceful liquescence, we were one body. He was in no hurry to get me into bed. "Is tonight the night?" I asked myself on our tenth date. He waited. I waited. The chemistry grew and finally exploded, and when we made love it went on for hours until, exhausted, I begged for mercy. He brought me coffee in bed, ran bath water for me, lit candles in the bathroom and looked at me with desire. I've never felt more beautiful.

It was never just sex with him. It was an exquisite, mind-blowing experience in ecstasy. He was fearlessly slow and deliberate as he devoted special attention to every little detail of my quivering body. He started with my face, caressing my cheeks, kissing my eyes, running his fingers through my hair, licking my lips, teasing me with short, mini kisses at first. Then he allowed his lips to linger sweetly, longer and longer on mine, holding my face between his hands as if it were a most precious jewel and must be held with the utmost care. Gently he nibbled on my ears and buried his face in the hollow of my neck, blowing warm air softly in all the right places.

He licked, he murmured, he nibbled. He told me I am beautiful. He said he found my body irresistible. He tantalized me with his hands and with his tongue, the hollow between my breasts, the crook of my elbow, the back of my neck. His mouth rested on my nipples, sucking gently, tweaking, flicking, and lingering long enough to incite the smoldering flame coursing down my being. Darting in between my legs, jetting from middle to infinity, passion had a mind of its own.

Exquisite torment held me in suspense and anticipation, slave to his conquering tongue, mesmerized by his exemplary skills, spellbound by his hypnotic instructions. Speechless, I could only moan. Throbbing with longing, aching for penetration, I waited while the words came, the sweet hot breath, the description of what he was going to do. The words drove me wild. "You want me, baby?" he asked. He relished the release of all inhibition, the loss of all control and my moan of desire.

"Say it," he said. "Say you want me."

"I want you. I want you. I want you."
"Say 'please.'"
"Please, please."
"Now?" he teased. "Do you want me now?"

He was a master at this. I drowned in bliss. I know there must be other men out there who are this willing to please a woman, but none of the other men I have known have been so willing to explore my needs and my body or to tell me all the things I long to hear. The most astonishing thing about Mike was that he had taken the time to learn how to please a woman. He knew how to play my body like a fine musical instrument, how to let me know that at that moment my pleasure was the most important thing in the world to him. He was never in a hurry. He loved the smells, the curves and the softness. When I asked about his expertise, he admitted that he read all the books he could find on the subject. He said he once was terrified of women and afraid of sex.

My heart cracked and bled when it was over, for a reason neither of us could have foreseen. He was, to say the least, an experience in passion such as I have never known before or since. In the silence of night or when I'm daydreaming during a quiet time, I conjure him up. I summon the memory, see him, smell the sweat and musk of him, and experience the essence of him. I'm grateful for that experience, and I move on knowing that I can cry because he died or rejoice because he lived.

Gladys

I'm eighty-six years old and my life still has its moments. I clean houses to supplement my social security, take care of my grandchild and relish any opportunity to dance.

I married young, to a dashing Navy man who pursued me and swept me off my feet. He was stationed at a base near where I lived and he got a part-time job where I worked. On his first day at work, he walked right up to me and said, "I want to take you out on a date." He was handsome. He was exciting. He was sure he wanted me.

No man had ever paid that much attention to me before. No man had ever said so many things that I wanted to hear. I was blissfully happy when we got married a few weeks later. He stayed in the Navy and we wrote letter after letter to each other, though it took weeks to get them. I waited with bated breath to hear from him.

I used to live for his love letters. Lots of women with husbands in the war went out with other men, but I never did. It was World War II and we all had to do our part. My part was to work hard and be faithful.

In the 1940s, every woman was well aware of how fleeting a serviceman's life on earth might be. I was definitely doing my part for my country, working in a factory, saving string and tinfoil, using my gas cards wisely. It was dangerous, it was exciting, it was expected.

When the war was over and my husband got out of the service, he seemed different. He was under foot all of the time. He wasn't fun anymore. He had changed. There was a melancholy about him and a sadness I couldn't reach. His laughter and lighthearted manner disappeared. He did not work. I tried understanding, anger, threats and pleading, but nothing worked. Life with him was no longer fun and exciting; it was drudgery. And he was drinking.

Our marriage fell apart. We stayed together for about three years until I could no longer financially support his habits. A few years later, I met and married the love of my life. It was wonderful—until the drinking started. He too had been in the war.

We adopted a child and both of us were crazy about him. I thought that having a child might end the drinking, but it did not. I wanted to stay with my husband because I loved my son so much. I couldn't. There were too many drunken fights, too much verbal abuse and too much irresponsibility. Being called all those shocking names—whore, slut, bitch—and being accused of all manner of things hurt me severely and left me hemorrhaging emotionally. It was the 1950s and there was no place for me to go. I had to keep on working and pretending to be happy until our son grew up. When I left, I vowed that I would never ever get married again.

This is what I wanted: a man in my life who could give me quiet support and understanding. Someone handy with tools. Someone who brought me gifts and cooked me a meal. Someone who was neat and clean, and smelled good. Someone who paid his own way. I would have liked it if he had complimented me, if he had offered to take me places, if he could have put me ahead of his drinking, if he wouldn't have forced me to lie for him when I called his work and said he was sick.

Sober, he was a good lover because I loved him. However, I would have enjoyed it more if he would have brushed his teeth and shaved before sex. I could not tolerate his advances when he was drunk, but we had sex anyway because I was afraid of him.

Men in the 1940s and 1950s had expectations and delusions of grandeur. They didn't much think about women's feelings or women's needs. Men expected to be the boss, to be served and serviced in appreciation for being the financial provider for the family. Even the men who did not financially support the family expected special treatment just for being a man. I stayed with my second husband for twenty-five years. Some years after I left him, he died. I didn't cry.

I have always worked. For many years I worked in a drug store. I turned to cleaning houses to make a living when I was 65 years old. My secret to having energy is to keep a positive attitude, never ever feel sorry for myself, laugh as often as possible and dance my heart out every Saturday night. I would rather dance than eat. My companion and steady dance partner is twenty years younger than I am. We dance, cook Sunday dinners together, and console each other when the chips are down.

When I get depressed, I just go find someone who needs help or a kind word and I give it to them. It makes me feel a lot better about myself. In retrospect, I know there was nothing wrong with me. I can see from earlier pictures that I was attractive. I never knew it. I always had to work hard and make sacrifices for my family.

I want to tell younger women to dwell on the good things in their lives. Look in the mirror and say to yourself, "I am beautiful." Say it repeatedly until you believe it. Never let a man be your whole life. Life is too short to feel sorry for yourself or entertain negative thoughts. Hold your head high. Do not let the media dictate your dreams. I am beautiful now and I like to wear sexy, silky underwear and gorgeous clothes. I love to dance and walk and dream and burn candles in my living room.

Helen

I had a husband and we shared life and an apartment for nineteen years. I never saw the other woman coming. One night my husband walked into the kitchen with the usual beer in his hand and watched while I was cooking supper. "Helen," he said, "I'm sick of our marriage. It hasn't been good for a long time. I've found a good woman who loves me."

Staggering a little, I blistered my hand on the open flame of my gas stove. I struggled to maintain my composure, but I couldn't. This was too much. I'd put up with his farts, his bellyaching, his clumsy lovemaking, his vulgar four letter words, his constant drinking—and now this. The fight was on. I threw a plate at him along with a stream of ugly words, accusations and threats. He hit me with his fists, opened the door and shoved me out into the wet, snowy wind. When I knocked and banged on the door, he threw my purse in the snow. He was an angry, drunk, disgusting, brutal man whom I trusted with my life. He was the only family I had.

Lost, stunned, hurt and confused, I stumbled around in the snow. "Where do I go? What do I do?" I thought. "I have no one." I wasn't allowed to have friends. Shocked and dazed, I staggered through the harsh cold night.

Should I beg him to let me back in? He wouldn't answer the door.

"What am I to do for money?" I thought. I searched my purse, and discovered I had enough money to buy a sleeping bag at Walmart.

I wiped the snow off a bench in the park and spent the first night lying there in agony. What had just happened? I was hungry. I was terrified. Where could I go? Who would help me? I was surprised to see so many homeless people on the street. I'd never noticed them before. Wandering up and down the streets the next day, I found my way to the homeless shelter. I was scared, I was horrified and I was lost. Who was I then? I was a homeless woman with the clothes on her back, hungry and needing a shower.

I fought off the dirty men leering at me in the shelter at night and wandered around in the daytime, looking for safe places to wait for the shelter to open for supper. Sometimes I sat across the street from my old apartment and wondered how I could get in and look in the refrigerator or grab some clothes. I was not able to get anything I owned from the apartment that was my home. I saw a strange woman going in and out. Was she using all my stuff? Why was he being so mean? Did he miss me at all? Were they living the good life? Maybe I should have drunk beer with my husband. Would he have loved me then? Where was God? Did He even care? Agonizing questions circled around in my brain like flies at a picnic. Long, lonely nights and endless days went on and on. I struggled to keep my sanity. I never felt safe. Little did I realize that I wouldn't feel safe again for years.

In the shelter I met Norman; he was big enough to protect me and I started lying down beside him at night. He seemed kind and gentle and I was so lost and alone. I was constantly fearful of being raped or hurt. We hung out together, wandering through the parks, sitting in the library, searching for food and warmth. We did this for a few months, then he said he liked me and wanted to get married. I did it, even though I didn't know if I was divorced or not.

Norman picked up a little work here and there. I searched for something to do to earn money, but employers wouldn't even talk to a grubby woman with ragged nails and murky hair. I had no work experience and no telephone number where they could reach me. We decided to hitchhike to Texas where his mom lived. He excitedly convinced me that there was hope for a home and a new life.

Hitchhiking is a demeaning, degrading, mortifying experience, and I was constantly dirty, exhausted and afraid. I started holding my breath and praying. When truckers picked us up and took us a few miles, I was humiliated and embarrassed. I never looked at them. I kept my head down. I know there is a God, but I didn't know if He knew there was a me.

We looked sloppy and dirty all the time. When we stopped at a cafe to eat, we had to show our money before we could get anything. Sometimes a church or a shelter gave us a food voucher. Using a food voucher to eat at a cafe brings out hateful comments from the waitresses and other customers. "Maggots, tramps and beggars" were just a few of the sneers we heard. "You are a disgrace," a woman spat at us as she walked by the place where we were sitting on a step, begging for food. Sometimes people with pity in their hearts bought us a meal or gave us a few bucks. I was too hungry to be mortified.

At night, we slept in a ditch, seeking one that was deep and full of grass. It actually felt safer in the ditch than in the parks or under the bridges, where there was the constant worry of being robbed or killed for the few possessions we carried.

Lying in the ditch, watching the cars go by, making ourselves as unseen as possible, we snuggled together to stay warm. We promised each other that when we got to Texas where his mother lived, all our troubles would be over. Norman told me about his mother, and I couldn't wait to meet her. I hadn't had a mother of my own for a long time. We planned what kind of jobs we wanted and dreamed about where we wanted to live.

One night we settled in a ditch right in the middle of a bed of red ants. Snuggling down in our zipped together sleeping bags, we were almost asleep when stinging and burning drove us to our feet. We shrieked obscenities, ripped off our clothes and ran naked through a wheat field, batting at our bodies, shaking our clothes in the wind and beating our sleeping bags against the ground. After that, we just kept on moving. I had ugly welts on my body.

Hiking into a truck stop, exhausted, dirty and hungry, I walked into the bathroom and tried to clean up a little. The bites from the red ants were itchy and swelling. A woman washed, then took lotion out of her purse and spread it on her hands. She ignored me while she used make-up out of a pink leather bag. The woman was maybe in her forties, close, I thought, to my age, and very stylish. I wondered what she would do if I asked to use her lotion on my chapped hands, sunburned face and red, swollen ant bites; if she noticed me, she didn't let on. Was I invisible? I hoped so, because I was ashamed. I pulled, rolled and folded as much toilet paper out of the stall as I could shove in my pockets and the waistband of my pants. Sometimes there was an extra roll of paper I could stick in my bedroll. I needed it because, to make matters worse, blood was running down my leg. Having a period is a monthly nightmare and a disaster when there is no money for supplies. There weren't even any paper towels in there. I would have to find some rags somewhere.

When I was in a city, if I could find a Salvation Army or a Goodwill store, I took some clothes off the rack, went into the fitting room and put them on. I left my old, dirty ones laying there. I put on as many clothes as I could so I would have rags when I needed them.

On the rare occasions when the cops took us to a motel room that was paid for by a church or the Salvation Army, I eagerly took advantage of the hot water, the soaps, lotions and shampoo. Sleeping in a bed with clean sheets felt like heaven. I hated it when we had to put our dirty clothes back on and truck on down the road. Before we left we checked out the dumpsters.

Only someone who has actually been homeless knows the mortification and feelings of disgrace that followed me everywhere I went, the feelings of ugliness when I looked at my faded red unkempt hair, my dirty, broken finger nails, the scratches and black and blue marks on my body, the hollowness of my eyes.

I learned a lot by watching other homeless people:
- Always sleep with your back to a wall if you can find one.
- Put everything you own under you when you sleep.
- Avoid eye contact.
- If a child is being beaten or a woman is being raped, look the other way.

- Don't complain. Other people have it worse than you do.
- When someone threatens you—leave.
- Eat a lot when you get the chance because it may be your last chance for a while.
- Carry store bags with you, so you will have something to put your dumpster finds in.
- Keep moving.

Bit by bit, we finally made it to Texas. We went back and forth from his mother's house to other areas, seeking jobs and trying to hang on to dreams that never materialized. The last time we went back to his mother's place there was a drunken blow-up, and our marriage ended with a gigantic blur of cursing and screaming. He was drinking up all of his mother's money. I couldn't live like this. His mother could have him.

Wandering the hot, dusty streets of a small Texas town, I noticed an abandoned gas station with the door hanging partially open. I went inside to rest. It was dim and dusty. The floors were concrete with dark ugly stains from random oil spills. The windows were caked with dust, cobwebs and dead flies, and did not let in much light or allow others to see inside. An old counter graced the front office and a broken chair sat against the wall. I hid behind the counter when someone walked too close to the window. The concrete floor was cold and hard, but at least it was shelter. The water was on and the bathroom contained a murky, filthy broken sink and a toilet, a blackish-orange bowl filled with slimy stuff, which worked.

It was my haven for three months. Alone in the dark and quiet I prayed and dreamed my dreams. Someday I would have a home. Someday this gnawing, throbbing, burning hunger for a home would be satisfied. I spent hours planning just how I would decorate it, with bright colors, lots of plants and books. It was always difficult to fall asleep but at least it was peaceful. No one next to me was getting raped or murdered.

Every day I scrambled for food and searched through dumpsters looking for blankets or rags to keep me warm at night. I found perfectly good loaves of bread and leftover casseroles. I woke up one night desperately ill, and decided that maybe the casseroles were not such a good idea. When there was a funeral, I went there to eat. Church potlucks were also good places for food. I kept my eyes down, searching the sidewalks, and sometimes I found coins or even dollar bills that I could use to buy a treat.

No one could know where I was staying. I lived in fear that someone would find me and hurt me or kick me out. Coming back at night, I constantly looked over my shoulder, and if I thought someone was following me, I went to the little park with the faded, broken-down merry-go-round, and sat beside a tree until it felt safe to go back to the station. It seemed strange to me that in three months of wandering, no one in the town questioned me or seemed even to notice me.

Loneliness and the search for my dreams drove me to move on. I could have died there. Sometimes I imagined what it would be like for someone to come to reclaim the station and, inside on the dirty concrete floor, find a dead woman in rags. I didn't dwell on the thoughts, though. They just crossed my mind when I was feeling desperate.

Hiking alone is genuinely terrifying. The hot wind and the dirty, sandy streets of Texas made my loneliness even more unbearable. In the first big town I came to, I asked for directions to the homeless shelter. After few days in there, I met Mark. He was in the Viet Nam War. He seemed nice. He had his own disability check, which is a very big plus. He drank a lot, but he was good to me. He couldn't stay at the shelter because of his drinking, so we drifted here and there, and I continued to dream about having a home of my own, a place where I could live and breathe with peace and comfort. It wouldn't have to be much, just mine. Home is a word that brought tears to my eyes and blood rushing to my heart. I wondered if I would ever have a home again.

We hitchhiked to a southern Texas resort town. It was warm and there was a carnival there. Praise God, we could work at the carnival! I worked hard and people seemed to like me. Mark, though, complained constantly and was completely unreliable. They fired him, but he would not leave me. So the police came, drove him twenty miles out on the highway, and left him there. This is something the Texas police do to homeless people all the time.

I stayed with the carnival and I got to know Ben. I really liked Ben. It was fun working there and I saved my money so I could go home. I had three hundred dollars that Ben kept for me. He wanted a home too, he said. Life was good. I had love, work and was getting closer to a home. When the carnival moved, we moved too.

One day in Tucson, Arizona, I woke up alone in our trailer. Ben was gone and so was all the money I had trusted him to hold. I had five dollars in my pocket. My heart was trashed and the cold chill of desolation moved in. The carnival was no longer fun. I couldn't face my life. I couldn't even get out of bed, and finally the carnival moved on and took my trailer with it, leaving me standing in an empty lot.

I found churches that provided meals three days a week. A woman at one of the churches helped me get on welfare. I wanted to live in an apartment, but I didn't have enough money for rent and the other things I needed, so I was still homeless. I desperately wanted to go home. I'd been on the road for several years, in the ditches, in the parks and under the bridges, each place as dangerous as the one before it.

I saw so much. Mothers with dirty, needy, uncontrollable, vacant-eyed children who often dance around in my nightmares. I went to missions, flophouses, run-down motels and soup kitchens. When I saw a rape, I turned my head. It is best not to notice, though my heart silently bled for the woman. I knew the pain was unbearable, the ripping and tearing of private parts, the humiliation, the disgrace and the sticky mess afterwards. When I was the one raped, I prayed and waited for it to be over. I have seen it all, and it is not pretty.

I was afraid I would die before I got to go home again. In some towns, the police picked me up like garbage. They gathered up a whole car full of derelicts (they called us this on their radios) and drove us out of town so the people in the next town could deal with us. In one town, I met and hooked up with Mac, a big hunk of a man who had his own RV. I thought it was my chance for a home. I had to trade sex for a roof over my head, but it was not so bad at first. He wanted to go to California so, late one night, we left Arizona.

I would have been safer on the street. He was a monster. My body ached and throbbed from the pain of the rapes and the beatings. He was very drunk most of the time. He threatened to take me out in the desert and kill me with his hunting knife. He laughed with evil, sinister sounds. He controlled my life, and when he went out for beer or food, he forced me to go with him. People looked at me with pity when they saw my black eyes and swollen face, but no one offered to help. One day when he was passed out on the couch, I sucked up all my courage and sneaked out. I called the police to come and arrest him. I did not dare to go near the RV after that, and everything I owned was in there.

Wandering around in California, I suffered from enormous, all-encompassing headaches that made me fall down. The headaches were from the beatings, I thought. My body felt old and weak. More and more my mind wandered back to the days when I was a child on the farm, and I remembered the spankings, beatings, ugly words and accusations I got from my mother.

Once I got a beating for asking about sex. I think my mother was a little crazy from losing my three brothers (one of them choked to death as a child). I remembered them all then, and sometimes I heard their voices. I wondered if I was going crazy. I was terrified, horrified and petrified all the time, with a cold sick dread that ate away at my bones and kept me constantly moving, perpetually looking over my shoulder. I tried to avoid the camps where homeless people steal from each other and a person could be murdered for a sleeping bag.

I did not know that, all those years, my first husband had been searching for me, not until I ended up in a town where my former best friend lived and I looked her up. I was embarrassed and dreadfully ashamed. I prayed that when she saw the dirt, the red chapped skin, the filthy hair and smelled the foul odor of my clothing, she would not send me away. She welcomed me with open arms and then yelled at me for not asking her for help. She told me that my former husband was constantly calling her. He'd been looking for me and he wanted me to come home. He would send me the money to take a bus. The grief, anguish and gratitude were all mixed up in my mind. I staggered and fell, crumbled in a mass of sobs. The sobs went on for hours. It had been ten years, and I had been in 26 states.

There was a new women and children's center in my hometown. It was comfortable and welcoming. My former husband was sober and had been for a few years. He wanted to make amends for his former behavior. He helped me get some of the things I needed, and took me to a doctor. A female pastor from a nearby church came to the shelter every week. Her words were like manna to my hungry soul, and she helped me to feel worthwhile. I had people in my life now that I could trust. The headaches continued to come and my thinking was confused from the head injuries, but I was safe. I was happy.

Thanks to some loving people from my church, I am in my own home with real furniture, and some of it is decorated just the way I imagined. I want what every woman wants. Love. I sought love everywhere except within myself. If I could tell a woman or a young girl anything, it would be that you must value and appreciate yourself. My life could have been so different if I had called the cops that cold, snowy night and put my husband out of the apartment instead of allowing him to do that to me. It didn't even occur to me.

Woman, stand up for yourself. Don't go anywhere thinking that it will be better than where you are now. Don't hook up out of desperation and at the first sign of abuse, seek help. I don't have a man in my life right now. I hope to meet one someday, somebody who is different from all the other men I have known. Only God knows if this will be.

Abra

I am 20-something, and a busy, complicated woman, who wants a simple thing: I want love. Not only do I want to love a man, but also to love children, friends, strangers, the world and life itself. Religion does not guide me, but when I open my heart to love, I can see my spiritual path. I am driven to love ever more deeply.

The start of a new relationship is intoxicating—beginning...falling...wanting....The possibilities of shared experience with someone lift me up and energize all my actions. I walk down the street with an extra spring in my step. I smile at people for no reason and everyday tasks take on more importance. I feel like a flower blooming, opening up, stretching my petals out, reveling in the sun and showering the world with my perfume. Love pours out of me for the old man in the wheelchair at the bus stop or the tattooed couple at the other table at the coffee shop. On my mind is whatever man has tapped into my deep well of feeling.

A new relationship becomes the amplifier for my love to expand further. No other cause has managed to unlock my heart in such a way. Love comes easily to me and it comes in a flood. I love even before I fall in love, but then my love always seems to knock people down and wash them away. All of my feelings are huge and unwieldy. When I am angry, I am a ball of fire that I struggle to extinguish before it ricochets around the room. When I am sad, I am a thunderstorm that threatens to drown me in the downpour, and when I am in love I am all giving, all present, all invested.

Loving may be easy, but its prerequisite—attraction and magnetism—sadly only grace me on rare occasions. I do not understand attraction. Why do I find one man beautiful and another man just ordinary? Physical looks only play a small part in luring me to a man. I find a man gorgeous when he has a certain spark, an air of confidence, a hint of sangfroid and a sexual vibe. I tend to be over-zealous in demonstrating my interest in a fellow. Perhaps I rob the man of the joy of the pursuit by being too easy to catch. Attraction renders me imposingly honest and my vulnerability is evident.

My many friends and family members have cautioned me about being consumed by love, counseling me to guard my heart. To them, avoiding pain is the important goal. However, I cannot live in fear of pain. Pain eventually fades, whereas the memory of a first kiss or of getting lost in a lover's gaze persists.

Pain and love first came to me together. My initial love was unbidden and forbidden; I was merely seeking the companionship of a kindred spirit. He was the first person through whom I came to know myself. I loathed him before I loved him, dismissed him before desiring him. One day I saw a spark inside of him that mirrored my own. Accidently I stumbled on myself and woke up to a new way of being. My identity was heated, hammered and hardened through our interactions. He introduced the elements of love, and with him I knew my first sweet taste of a lover's kiss.

The bitter truth of our relationship is that it has to be secret. No one we know would approve of our being together. There is no pain to rival that of having to hide a beautiful love. My first lesson in love is that no one can tell you who is right for you, so you had better follow your own heart. Loving, risking and longing are such sweet and sour emotions.

Before I ever loved a man, I had crushes on boys. Now I cannot comprehend what I liked about a single one of my childish crushes. I can only remember them now with embarrassment. Regretfully, I admit that elements of a crush are present in all of my other relationships as well. After attraction leads to dating, then to relationships, I sometimes discover that I have no idea why I am with the man who is holding my hand. Loving love itself can be so delightful that it is easy to stay in a relationship just to keep a grip on it even when you can no longer endure your partner's behavior. I think this is the true meaning of *settling*.

I have a theory that we learn how to love just as we learn how to play. Children engage in parallel play before they connect with each other. My first relationship felt like this; I love him, he loves me; we sort of adapt to each other but we never really look in the same direction together. Our love flows in parallel lines, never uniting in any meaningful way beyond the initial lust. This is true of most of my relationships.

Everyone makes love out to be something mystical, but couldn't it be as simple as being inextricably tied to your self-identity? I lost myself in love, and when my relationship ended, I struggled to find myself again. As a result, I gained some additional insight into what I want. After having a hidden love, I now crave recognition and social acceptance. Everything about a new partner seems to be perfectly matched to me: we want the same things, have the same values, each complimenting the other in our differences. So why does my heart get broken again and again?

Now that years have passed, I can see that I ignore who my partner is and focus on what he can bring to the relationship. Out of my loneliness and desire to have a family, I have a tendency to fool myself. I hook up, we play house for a while until he realizes that he is not happy or in love with me. Even though I know I do not love him, I take the breakup hard. I kick myself for never being the one to recognize reality. Being single seems unbearable. I want a family so much. I mourn for a while, and then my inner Pollyanna pipes up and reminds me that now I have an opportunity to find someone with whom I am truly well matched. But I now pay attention to incompatibilities and avoid settling for less than I want.

I am on a sexual time-out. Even though I have been lost in love, blind to my own desires, I can stay true to myself when I love. Leaving sex out of the picture makes my vision clearer. No longer do I expect my life to be completed by another human being. It is so much better to love a person who is whole and separate from me. My mistakes were necessary; there was no way to avoid them on my journey to love. Sometimes being single must be embraced and even reveled in to be a better partner.

At this time, I need to explore a much-neglected side of myself: my sexual self. Emotions seem to scare people, and mine are no exception. People tell me to seek anger management assistance, to take drugs to manage grief and to resist falling in love too fast. I have tried to heed their advice, but when I do, I feel I have denied my soul. No one has ever suggested I feel more strongly, more intensely. In order to be my best self, I feel I need to learn more about what inspires my strong feelings. I need to learn how to love in small parts, letting each build upon the other. I need to distinguish hormonal lust from heart-felt love.

I am experiencing casual dating for the first time. Between relationships, I have often sought out the physical comfort of a man's touch. I like to think it was not out of desperation and despair, but perhaps it was. However, I pride myself that my sexual consolations were never found in a drunken stupor. I acted by choice and loved my partners for the moment and for the comfort they brought. I picked men whose humanity I could respect and who would give me what I needed. I am incredibly fortunate to have had very few negative sexual experiences, and even fewer regrets. I like men. Men are what make life worth living.

I meet many men I like, but not enough to date them long term. I respect them enough not to insult them by letting them use me. I now notice men who previously would not have caught my eye. Physical looks are less important to me. I look for strength and inner beauty. Meeting my own sexual needs ironically gives me a much better sense of what I want from a husband. Having sex without my emotional needs exploding all over an unsuspecting partner gives me a little control over my emotional floodgate. No longer do I *fall* in love helplessly. Now I *jump*.

I have learned that love is much more of a conscious choice than a lightning bolt or a cupid's arrow. I know now that having standards and expectations for your partnerships is actually quite wise. Just as Pandora opened the box to let loose all the evils in the world, I am releasing my loving self on the world.

Somehow I manage to hang onto hope. Time after time, the man I love leaves me. My first love left me three times before he finally stayed gone. More than once, after years of dating, a man tells me that he hoped I was the one and has now realized I am not. The boyfriend with whom I had breathtaking and amazing sex just did not bother to call one day, then faded into oblivion.

I know myself better now. I understand that I have not demanded consideration and respect. I do not love with any thought of an end. I want love to last forever. My ocean of tears, when love doesn't last, nearly drowns me. Through it all, I learned that huge feelings don't destroy me, they expand me. There is a pendulum: the more feeling I allow myself to experience, the bigger the backlash when that feeling is relinquished. When I love a partner, I love them completely and when the relationship ends, I lose my way of life because I have molded myself to his needs, and given myself away. It is challenging for me to achieve a great height of love without losing myself.

I cannot tell anyone else how to do it. All I can tell you is that I have found it is possible. I needed all my different experiences and heartbreaks to get me here. It has been trial and error all the way.

Loving in vain no longer feels like love to me. It is imperative to my sanity to be able to move on. The end of one love must therefore be the beginning of something better. Every man I have loved or shared an intimate moment with has added something to my life. I will carry the memory of these relationships always. With artistic flourishes, my tears of heartbreak wash away the pain of old loves, leave me free of bitterness and prepare the way for my heart to risk loving again.

I recently confessed my feeling for a man with whom I have been spending an increasing amount of time. He admitted he is attracted to me and there were many signs our relationship was growing. We spent more and more time together and had great sex. The physical intimacy seemed to distress him, though. After the testosterone was dispersed, he was visibly remorseful. His religious views were in conflict with his carnal desires. It saddened me that the beautiful acts of intimacy we shared created deep pang of guilt for him. We acknowledged to each other that this relationship could not lead to anything permanent. This ended our friendship. As patronizing as this might sound, the older I get the easier it is to say goodbye.

When a man fails to feel as strongly as I do and I'm denied the chance to love, my soul seems to wilt. I feel like the genie in the bottle, waiting to be freed. I am not afraid to feel the bumps on the road of life. My arms are wide open for the range of experiences that are possible.

Love is my spiritual quest. I love life in all its flavors. I am grateful for life, for love, for passion and even for pain. I know I am not alone in wanting the opportunity to love another person. I continue to seek. I know that the search for love permeates our culture. There are many women who, like me, have allowed love to consume a lot of their energy. I am truly blessed to have had so many loves, and I am grateful for the experiences and the love I have received. I am no longer angry.

Natasha

I was born to a teenage mother who already had one child. My parents married after I was born and divorced when I was in the first grade. The same year my father moved out, my beloved grandmother died.

My dad was an extremely depressed alcoholic and I rarely saw him, but when I did see him, I always ended up feeling guilty. He often called me on the telephone when he was drinking. He cried and said he missed me, and I was always trying to take away his hurt. He praised my mother to me, never put her down, but continually reminded me that it is a woman's job to take care of her man.

Mom had to work hard. She always held down two jobs. She went out on dates sometimes. When she got pregnant, she married my stepfather. My brothers and I always made fun of him because he came and tried to establish new rules. No way would we let that happen! My stepfather whined to me and asked me to tell him that he was a good person. Then he would call my father names and say mean things about him. Of course, I stuck up for my father and the fight was on.

Mom told me not to follow in her footsteps. She persistently and annoyingly nags me about taking better care of myself than she does. She said not to have children until I am at least thirty years old. Though it was not conscious, I did have my first child at the age of thirty.

My mother was a beautiful woman and she gave me some very strong messages. Women can do everything. Single women have it best because you don't have to ask a man for anything. Women are stronger than men are and more resilient. Women can get through anything and still serve dinner with a smile to protect the kids. She told me to keep my feelings to myself. My mom did not express emotions. I never saw her cry. Now, when I try to express emotions, I do not know if I do it well because it doesn't come easy to me.

The only conversation I ever had with my mom about sex went like this: "There is a book about sex in my nightstand. You can read it any time you want." I never read the book. I learned about sex in the fifth grade from a seventh grader who talked me into going down into his basement with him, and again in high school when a home economics teacher taught us about birth control.

In high school I was a good student and made good grades. I was a very responsible girl at home, even though I felt like I was carrying a heavy and ominous emotional load. Alcohol helped. I drank with the explicit intention of getting drunk two to four nights a month. It lifted my burdens some. My mom was very low-key about it. All my friends liked to come to my house because my mom wasn't into rules.

I only had one boyfriend in high school and whenever we dated, no matter where we went I took my books and studied. I had a crush on one boy, but he told my friends that he wouldn't touch me with a ten-foot pole. When I heard this, I was devastated. My hopes of a normal relationship were shattered.

I wasn't sexually active until I graduated from high school. During that summer I went out on a date. We got drunk. My date wanted sex and I did not want to do it, so he raped me. During the rape, I left my body for a while. When it was over, I got out of the car and walked home. I called my best friend but I never told anyone else. I was too overwhelmed with shame.

In college, I started drinking more and became very promiscuous. I sometimes woke up bleary-eyed in some guy's dorm room and didn't know where I was. I loved attention. I loved the challenge of walking into a party, looking around, and deciding which guy I was going to seduce. It was a game, and I always got the guy, even when he was with someone else.

In college, I received a letter from a girl in a correctional facility. She said she was my father's child. I talked with her on the telephone a couple of times, but we could find nothing in common except Dad. One day my mom came to visit me at school and she had a young, good-looking guy with her. It turns out she had a child before I was born and gave him up for adoption. My world is continually more complex and confusing.

The hangovers lasted longer. To get away from it all I moved to Palm Springs, California, and became the manager of a luxury restaurant. For a couple of years I maintained a fairly healthy relationship, and it was giving me time to heal and to sort out my life. The man I was with was gentle, compassionate and concerned about me. He helped me rebuild and establish some strong values. Slowly, over time, I became aware of a need to make a contribution to society, and I gained a new realization that connectedness, family, people and nature are all that matter.

It was time to do something bigger with my life, so I joined the Peace Corps. Somewhere in India, I met my future. I was at a party and he asked me to dance. When we danced, it felt just right. I felt connected, linked in some subtle, new way. We exchanged email addresses and the rest is history.

He says that for him it was love at first sight. I finally understand what people mean when they talk about soul mates. We have similar views on the world, on family and on spirituality. The only difference between us is stuff—I don't think we have much, and he thinks we have too much. We do have some differences that stem from our different cultural backgrounds, but they are not insurmountable and sometimes they are even funny.

Spiritually, I believe that God is everywhere and in everything. I do not call myself a Christian, although I believe that Christ set an example for how people should live. I believe He was deified, but I do not believe that I have to go through Him to have a relationship with God. I believe that God speaks to our heart directly and if I listen, I will be doing what God wants me to do. With God in my heart, I follow my heart. I have learned that if I go with the flow of things, opportunities just fall in my lap. I believe the critical things for happiness are relationships, spirituality and knowing when to let go. I have everything I want.

Connie

What do I want?
I am a woman
I want my soul to be awakened by love
I want my heart to be joined in sacredness
with love and passion
I want a flower when I awaken on a winter day
A kiss in the moonlight
A glance across a room
that can bring life or death
I long for the slow, slow touch of my lover's hand
that makes the world stop
Holding its breath
until he presses his lips to mine
I want the holy moment of joy
of giving up all that is not me
to birth all that is in me
I want the intimacy of the sea on my body
The moonlight whispering
on my upturned face
I want to be consumed by grace
on a mountain top
I long for depth
For connection
My world rests on being seen
Look closely, see me now
in all my glory, my tragedy
my regrets, my frets
Look closely--look closely
I am here.

Postscript

On a scale of 1 to 10, what's your chance of getting what you want?

People entering a new relationship are excited, optimistic and giddy. New love hits the brain with feelings of euphoria not unlike that produced by cocaine.[5] This can only last while everything is new. Unfortunately, in a short time the burps, farts, warts and differences appear. It's what you do after this discovery that determines whether the relationship will last or, if it does last, whether it will be fulfilling or emotionally sapping.

I know people who have been together for years who have managed to keep their love alive through many hardships and the peculiar ordeals of life. What is their secret? They've learned that good relationships don't just happen. It takes an effort on the part of both partners. They understand in a special way that when you really love someone, giving that person something that you know would make them feel happy and fulfilled is a privilege. When a relationship works, it is because the partners have learned how to relate and give to each other.

As adults, we have learned our relationship skills by observing and experiencing the behavior of the parents who raised us. If you were lucky and you had

---

[5] Nordqvist, Christian, *Journal of Sexual Medicine*, October 27, 2010, and www.medicalnewstoday.com.

"good" people in your life, people who taught you some healthy living skills, then you are a step ahead of many others when it comes to establishing a healthy relationship. Some of us grew up in homes where the examples before us were destructive and discouraging. For those who learned as a child a harsh lesson about avoiding confrontation, the thought of conflict turns them to Jell-O. Many parents teach children to ignore feelings of discomfort around abuse or differences, and to turn a blind eye to things that are hurtful. Some of us are taught to accept excuses for bad behavior, and in some families anything goes as long as there is a good enough excuse.

If you want to have a quality relationship, it is imperative to discover which lessons you learned are now governing your life. You can overcome the negative lessons from your past. You have the right and the obligation to have the best life possible. Don't throw it away. Don't live a half-life and do get the help you need to make positive changes. Do not be fainthearted about asking for details about the early life of anyone with whom you are in relationship. And don't dismiss or minimize emotionally unhealthy behavior on the part of a friend or mate.

To be part of a couple is a superb gift of life. Never take for granted this opportunity to be with someone who is choosing to be with you. Share stories of early childhood and family beliefs. Discuss differences respectfully. Learn how to fight fair. Learn to listen well and to express your feelings with affection. Above all, learn the arts of gratitude and apology. In a healthy relationship trust is a vital ingredient. In a healthy relationship neither person ever lies, not even by omission, threatens abandonment or tries to intimidate the other. Complete honesty is vital, and you can learn how to be honest without demoralizing your partner.

If you are married and have been for several years and find yourself in a negative rut, don't waste time with resentment and regrets, even if you are in an unhealthy relationship. It's not too late to seek a quality connection with your partner. And it is never too late to have a quality sex life. People of sixty, seventy, even eighty, often have a better sex life than people who are much younger.

Give the one you care about every opportunity to grow with you. If she/he refuses to cooperate, after you have done everything you can to make the relationship healthy, you have a decision to make. Whether you decide to stay or go, do it with a lot of prayer.

If you are dating, be diligent in examining closely the character of the person you are dating. Be true to your own scruples, principles and beliefs. Turn in your crystal ball and go for all the information you need to determine if this is the right relationship for you. Never duck the hard questions. Don't waste your time on someone who talks down to you or treats you shabbily. Make sure his character matches his words. Know that if you are not honest in the relationship, you make healthy connection impossible. If you lie, cheat and steal, you will expect your partner to do the same. And you will get what you expect.

No matter if you are dating, married or cohabitating, a relationship only works when both people know what they want and are headed in the same general direction. It only works when it is reciprocal. If there is no mutual give and take, one partner ends up feeling exploited.

Some men have personality disorders that make healthy relationship impossible. You can distinguish a personality disorder from simple ignorance this way: If it is ignorance, your partner will make every effort to meet your needs when you tell him what they are. If it is a personality disorder, your partner will promise change but will not be able to follow through.

When you think about your partner first, your relationship will thrive, but only if you do it from a place of security in your own value and worth, only if you do it because putting your partner first gives you a sense of personal satisfaction. When you deny yourself and put your partner first from a place of fear or guilt or because you are trying to keep the peace, things don't go so well.

If your love is selfish and self-seeking, you will be more concerned about your ego and your sense of comfort than about pleasing your partner. People with low self-esteem sometimes think that giving in to a partner's request makes them less of a person, while people with healthy self-esteem delight in making their partner happy.

Make an effort to acquire good communication skills. Learn how to appreciate, negotiate and commiserate. Find out what your partner wants, urge him/her to be honest, and work as a couple to make sure both of you move toward what you want. Ask, "On a scale of one to ten, how important is what you want—to you?" Anything above a seven means you just do it— providing it is not physically harmful or detrimental to your own well-being. You do it, considering it a great adventure and an opportunity to show your partner how important he or she is to you.

These are the four things you need for a strong relationship:
1. Patience.
2. Lots of appreciation.
3. A good sex life.
4. Humility.

Now, you, the reader, get to write your own ending to this book. Take a good look at yourself and answer these questions:

- What's your story?
- What do you want?
- Are you content?

Spend some time contemplating or meditating on your answers. Make a determination to welcome every opportunity to learn and grow. And know that there is one thing you have complete power over, and that is your attitude. Life happens. You get to decide how to approach it and what you want to think about it. You get to decide how to live it.

About the Author
Evelyn Leite, MHR, LPC

Evelyn Leite, MHR, LPC and author, has 30 years of experience in the addiction and mental health fields. Noted for her humanitarian work, in 2008 she was inducted into the South Dakota Hall of Fame and is widely regarded for her seminars in multicultural counseling and education. She has designed and implemented relationship programs throughout the United States, and is noted for her success in the treatment of trauma resolution, anxiety, and depression. She has authored a dozen books for publishers including Hazelden Publications and the (former) Johnson Institute, as well as in numerous magazine and newspaper articles.

Feedback

I welcome your letters and feedback to this book. Please email me at evelyn@evelynleite.com, or you may write to me at Post Office Box 9702, Rapid City, South Dakota 57709.

CPSIA information can be obtained
at www.ICGtesting.com
Printed in the USA
BVHW03*1624251018
530278BV00003B/47/P

9 781945 333064